LES ENFANTS TERRIBLES

T0347980

OLIVER LANSLEY

Les Enfants Terribles

Collected Plays

THE TERRIBLE INFANTS ·
ERNEST AND THE PALE MOON
THE VAUDEVILLAINS

OBERON BOOKS
LONDON

WWW.OBERONBOOKS.COM

First published in 2011 by Oberon Books Ltd
521 Caledonian Road, London N7 9RH
Tel: +44 (0) 20 7607 3637 / Fax: +44 (0) 20 7607 3629
e-mail: info@oberonbooks.com
www.oberonbooks.com

A catalogue record for this book is available from the British Library.

The Publisher is grateful to the photographers and designers for
permission to reproduce the images in this book.

PB ISBN: 978-1-84943-163-7
E ISBN: 978-1-84943-725-7

Cover design by Samuel Wyer
Front cover photography © David G Monteith-Hodge
Inside front cover photography © Graham Lewis
Inside back cover photography © Karen Scott
Back cover photography © Alex Stephens

Visit www.oberonbooks.com to read more about all our books and to
buy them. You will also find features, author interviews and news of
any author events, and you can sign up for e-newsletters so that you're
always first to hear about our new releases.

Contents

INTRODUCTION

I'm thrilled to be collaborating with Oberon on this collection and really excited to finally see these works in print.

I hope these three pieces serve as a fitting collection, both as stand-alone productions but also as a body of work from my theatre company Les Enfants Terribles.

It has taken a while for these scripts to be published as it has previously been said that they are so closely associated with Les Enfants Terribles productions that they would not work separately in a published form.

Thankfully Oberon viewed this as a virtue as opposed to an obstacle, so in acknowledgement of that we have attempted to embrace the connection and offer this volume up as a companion piece to our productions of the work.

Within this book I have included various production photos and design sketches, as well as contributions from key creatives involved in the productions.

This is by no means to suggest that this is the way it 'should' be done, or to offer any kind of instruction, but merely to offer up an insight into our process and how we went about transforming these pieces into productions.

I hope should anyone else attempt to produce these scripts in the future they will feel empowered to explore the source material and bring it to life in their own unique way.

For me putting these works together in one volume forms a very fitting collection as I have always seen them as a thematic trilogy. Each piece is an exploration of storytelling; from children's stories, to scary stories, to stories set to music.

I hope you enjoy reading this work half as much as we have enjoyed devising and performing it over the years.

ACKNOWLEDGEMENTS

I would like to thank every single person who has in any way been involved in the productions mentioned in this book. I wish I could have listed you all individually but it would have filled up a whole other volume!

I would also like to thank anyone who has ever been involved in a Les Enfants Terribles production and everyone who has ever been to see one of our shows.

This company has been built on collaboration, favours, belief, blood, sweat, tears, late nights, broken down vans, scout huts, lots of alcohol and people giving up their time and money and anything else they have to make things happen. I salute each and every one of you.

I will never be able to thank my family enough for the incredible support they have offered me over the years. None of this would have been possible without them and still to this day they are always there when I need them. This book is dedicated to them. Thank you and I love you.

Also on behalf of all the other 'Enfants' I would like to thank their families as I know they have all been an incredible support to the company and our work.

James Seager, my partner in crime. The work recorded in this book would not have happened without you – it's been a journey! We've been through a lot, highs, lows and everything in between and made it out the other side…just. Thank you for the support, the friendship, the hard work and the stories we've accumulated over the years – Here's to many more.

Tomas Gisby – 'It's been a hell of a ride' and I will miss you sincerely as a fellow Enfant. Over the years you have given us so much; as a composer, a performer, a designer, a producer and as a friend, not to mention many other guises no doubt. Our work would not be what it is without you – It has been a pleasure working alongside you all these years.

Sam Wyer – You're a genius, it's always a joy to collaborate with you and watch your creations grow. You are officially worth the effort!

Rachel Dawson – Thank you for putting up with my madness. Your talent, inspiration and contribution to all three of these pieces was invaluable. You're one of the most talented people I know. Thank you and I love you.

Jessica Cooper at Curtis Brown, thank you for being a fantastic agent and a great friend, you're always there to help me figure out what to do and to help me deal with the bumps along the way.

All the pieces in this book received their official premiere at one of The Pleasance venues in Edinburgh. I would like to say a huge thank you to Anthony Alderson, Emma Bettridge, Cass Mathers and all the wonderful staff at The Pleasance for believing in us, supporting us and allowing us to present our work in a variety of weird and wonderful ways.

Les Enfants Terribles can only exist with the invaluable support from our audience and fans.

To become a 'friend' of the company or to join our mailing list please visit our website:

www.lesenfantsterribles.co.uk

Company History

'As the name of his company suggests, Oliver Lansley of Les Enfants Terribles has actually found that winning formula of talent, charm and absolute irreverence – think, really cool top-of-the-class kid.' *The Stage*

'Razor-sharp theatre group Les Enfants Terribles' (*The Telegraph*) are dedicated to creating original, innovative and exciting theatre that challenges, inspires and entertains. We are constantly pushing ourselves to explore and develop new techniques and methods to tell stories whilst – at the heart of our work – always remaining accessible to our audience and ever-growing fan base. Born out of genuine passion and excitement for creating theatre, we are always keen to find new ways of immersing ourselves and our audiences into the weird and wonderful worlds created by our shows.

Founded by Artistic Director Oliver Lansley in 2001, the company has continued to grow and receive consistent critical acclaim, been nominated for and won top industry awards, and established a large and loyal following for its original and unique work. The company has performed productions to thousands of people all over the world including theatres in Poland, Czech Republic, Dubai, Norway, Singapore and has toured extensively all over the UK.

Long time collaborators James Seager and Tomas Gisby came on board as associate producers to help run the company in 2005 and 2007 respectively.

Since 2001 the company has gone from performing in 50-seat venues on a shoestring budget to working consistently in large-scale venues, building a considerable critical and commercial following and touring the globe with its fresh and innovative productions. Les Enfants Terribles have now built a reputation for being one of the most visually exciting British theatre companies working today.

'Is there anything Les Enfants Terribles can do wrong? Missing a show by Les Enfants Terribles would constitute somewhat of a sacrilege.' *Hairline*

The Company's inceptive production, *West*, began with a sell-out run in London's Docklands before being asked to transfer to The Assembly Rooms for the 2002 Edinburgh Festival where it won the Herald Devil Award and *The Times* 'Critic's Choice'.

The Germinator	(Assembly Rooms, Edinburgh Festival 2003) 5 Star 'Hairline Highlight' winner: *'Takes theatre beyond mere entertainment...'*
Bedtime Stories	(Landor Theatre, London & Gilded Balloon, Edinburgh Festival 2004) 5 Star 'Top Ticket': *'Definitely one of this year's 'must sees.'*
Immaculate	(Gilded Balloon, Edinburgh Festival 2005. Old Red Lion, London 2006. International and Domestic Tour 2006) 5 Star 'Critic's Choice': *'Genuinely a laugh-a-minute, with some real strokes of comic genius.'*
	Published by Nick Hern Books and listed as one of the top ten-selling plays in Samuel French London in 2010.

The Infant　　　　　(Gilded Balloon, Edinburgh Festival
　　　　　　　　　　　　& Old Red Lion, London 2006.
　　　　　　　　　　　　International Tour 2007)
　　　　　　　　　　　　5 star 'Critic's Choice':
　　　　　　　　　　　　*'An amazing play; The Infant is excellent
　　　　　　　　　　　　on every level, and there are not enough words
　　　　　　　　　　　　to praise all of its qualities.'*

The Terrible Infants (Pleasance, Edinburgh Festival 2007.)
　　　　　　　　　　　　The show has since toured, on and off,
　　　　　　　　　　　　both domestically and internationally,
　　　　　　　　　　　　including performances at the Esplanade,
　　　　　　　　　　　　Singapore, The Southbank centre, London
　　　　　　　　　　　　and two returns to the Edinburgh Festival in
　　　　　　　　　　　　2008 (Udderbelly) and 2010 (Pleasance Grand).
　　　　　　　　　　　　5 star 'Critic's choice':

　　　　　　　　　　　　Winner of: The Argus Angel award, Latest 7
　　　　　　　　　　　　Best Children's Event Award, Fringe
　　　　　　　　　　　　Review's Outstanding Theatre Award and
　　　　　　　　　　　　Fringe Report's Best Entertainment Award.
　　　　　　　　　　　　'Magical, this is storytelling as it should be.'

Ernest and the Pale Moon (Pleasance, Edinburgh Festival 2009.
　　　　　　　　　　　　Domestic tour 2010)
　　　　　　　　　　　　5 star 'Critic's choice'

　　　　　　　　　　　　Winner of: 'Darkchat' Award, 'Hairline
　　　　　　　　　　　　Highlight' Award. The Stage 'Must See
　　　　　　　　　　　　Show'. Total Theatre Award Nominee.
　　　　　　　　　　　　'A gloriously gothic production.'

The Vaudevillains　　(Latitude Festival & Pleasance, Edinburgh
　　　　　　　　　　　　Festival 2010. Charing Cross Theatre 2011)
　　　　　　　　　　　　5 star 'Critic's choice'
　　　　　　　　　　　　'A perfect miniature musical.'

In the future, the Company hope to continue to produce work that captures people's imaginations and to keep building our reputation as one of the most fresh and exciting theatre companies around.

　　　*'A talented company with a very sure sense of its own distinctive
　　　　　　　　　　　storytelling style.' Guardian*

Oliver Lansley

Oliver is a writer, actor and director and the founder and Artistic Director of Les Enfants Terribles Theatre Company. A past winner of 4Talent's Multi-Talented Award and Broadcast Hotshot (2008), he has worked extensively in theatre, film and television.

As a writer Oliver is a published playwright and writes all the company's output; his play *Immaculate* was recently listed in the top ten best-selling plays at Samuel French London and his work has been translated into several different languages across the world.

His television work includes BBC2's critically acclaimed comedy *Whites* – 'a perfect example of the modern sitcom' (*The Times*) starring Alan Davis, Katherine Parkinson and Darren Boyd which he co-created and wrote. He also co-created and wrote the Rose D'or-nominated ITV2 series *FM* – 'the greatest radio station comedy since *Frasier*' (*Metro*), starring Chris O'Dowd and Kevin Bishop.

As an actor, Oliver has performed in numerous theatre productions from Eddy in Berkoff's *Greek* at The Riverside Studios to Puck in *A Midsummer Night's Dream* at Pendley Shakespeare Festival. He regularly tours internationally with the company's shows; most recently *The Terrible Infants* in which he played the Narrator, *Ernest and the Pale Moon* in which he played Ernest and *The Vaudevillains* in which he played The Compere.

His television credits include *Whites*, *Holby City*, *FM*, *Doctors* and *EastEnders*.

THE TERRIBLE INFANTS

Based on stories conceived

by Oliver Lansley and Sam Wyer

For Charlie, Archie & Poppy

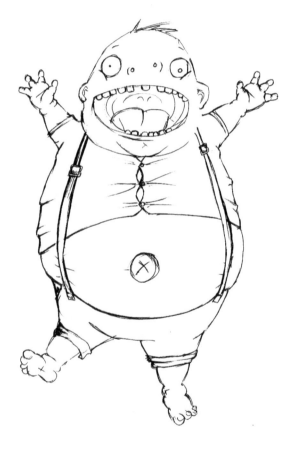

'Tumb', character sketch – Sam Wyer

Foreword

The Terrible Infants is my homage to all the great children's stories I remember from my youth. Be it Roald Dahl or The Brothers Grimm, the stories I remembered most were always the ones that scared and excited me, the ones that challenged me.

The Terrible Infants was about exploring that most basic form of storytelling. Though it is important to note that we never set out to create a 'children's show', rather a show that made grown-ups feel like children. A small but fundamental distinction!

The copy you read here is in script form – in line with our production of the piece. But it is worth noting that when we started the rehearsal process we were working with the stories in prose form, based upon stories originally conceived by myself and Illustrator/Designer Sam Wyer.

We then went about dividing them up and creating the full production and narrative around them.

In line with the content of the piece our process was very childlike – we approached the stories like children in a back garden, rooting through a dressing-up box, looking for bits of junk to try and help us find interesting and inventive ways to tell our stories. This approach very much coloured the production as a whole and I think that sense of 'play' is a vital ingredient in the success of this piece.

It's pure old-fashioned storytelling – for all the effects and puppets and music that we involved in the piece we always wanted to know that underneath it all, when everything was stripped back, it could still work and engage in its simplest form – someone on a stage telling the audience a story.

I've been lucky enough to have toured the world with *The Terrible Infants*, playing to all different age groups and often to audiences where English isn't even their first language and I think it is the simplicity mentioned above that has made that possible – everyone loves a good story.

Oliver Lansley

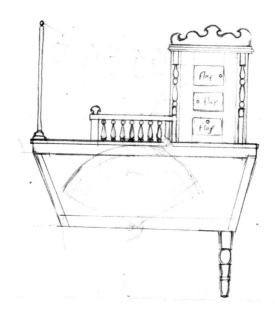

Cart concept ideas – Sam Wyer

Designing The Terrible Infants

The creation of *The Terrible Infants* was an exciting and immersive experience. Once the stories had been written we spent a very enjoyable weekend with a group of friends and several sheds full of dustbins, prams, bicycles and other delicious junk, where we began to explore the texts.

Each story took a different form, from walk-around performances to slapstick-filled sketches.

This process gave us our starting point and created the language of 'proppetry' that continued into the final show, where the junk elements remained evident. Tumb, for instance, I created using dustbin lids, an appropriate object for our incrementally obese opening character, and Mingus was built on an old crash helmet, worn on top of the head to exaggerate his strange angular expressions.

Through the devising process that followed, the physical development of each character was stripped back based on their exact function within the story, for example Tumb became merely a head and a stomach. This allowed the skill of the actors to integrate seamlessly with the character itself, blurring the line between puppet and performer.

This feeling is consistent throughout the show, where slick physical performance and direction work alongside props and puppets, meaning performers barely take a breath or even leave the stage but put on an incredible show.

Costuming the cast was a lot of fun too, and was led very much by their characters which came to light through the devising process. Like the rest of the show it was visually very cobbled together, with each costume consisting of numerous bits and pieces reclaimed from charity shops or constructed from old clothes.

This toy-box aesthetic was very important to us as a company to inspire a sense of nostalgia and playfulness which was the starting point for the stories themselves.

The Cart, as the central object in the show, is used in multiple ways, and as a touring company gives us a structural focus without an outer structural set, allowing the show to play venues as diverse as a five-metre tent to a fifteen-metre stage. It was also very important to the nomadic, storytelling quality we wanted the show to encapsulate.

Since we began touring the show, the audience and venues have grown in size but the stories and performances have maintained their intimate quality. The only real changes in the visual style have been to allow them to read slightly better in larger venues and with the growing lighting palettes we have had at our disposal.

That said, we still have a few tricks up our sleeve and a few stories to expand the world we have created!

Many thanks to everyone who has helped us create this incredible show, especially to my Mother and Father, Nick and Trish Wyer.

Samuel Wyer, Designer

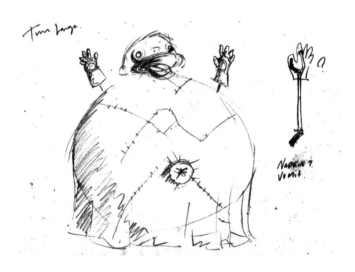

'Tumb' concept drawing – Sam Wyer

Cart design details – Sam Wyer

Character sketches – Sam Wyer

'Mingus' concept drawing – Sam Wyer

THE TERRIBLE INFANTS
2007 - 2010

THE EVENING STANDARD ★ ★ ★ ★ ★
The Terrible Infants is a beautifully realised slice of vaudevillian puppet theatre and crawls with characters that could have escaped from Lewis Carroll's waste paper basket... a woe-strewn, Struwwelpeter-esque revue of twisted cautionary tales.

METRO ★ ★ ★ ★ ★
It's like giving your inner child an enormous sack of sweets and a cuff round the ear: ever-ballooning glutton Tumb and vanity-stricken rag doll Linena would each have Tim Burton writhing with glee... Wildly lyrical, darkly camp and musically adept, performing company Les Enfants Terribles also boasts a gorgeously lo-fi eye for detail... Polished till it shines and played beautifully by a cast looking like naughty toys that have escaped from the nursery... scattered moments of sharply choreographed physical slapstick keep the needle pointed firmly at fun as they blend delicate songs and artfully inventive props with witty narration...

THE STAGE – CRITIC'S CHOICE
Song, rhyme, puppets and slapstick make for a great romp via Les Enfants Terribles' tall tales about terrible children... What happens in between the terrible tales is just as captivating, as the travelling band of players joke, jibe and gyrate with each other. Witty and hummable, the songs are written and played by Tom Gisby and Neil Townsend on a Heath Robinson-like array of instruments. Sam Wyer's set is another star of the show: an appealing clutter that includes a side-show on wheels... There is a refreshingly modern twist to all of this that does not detract from its gothic morality, so taking the spirit of Struwwelpeter, Edward Gorey and Roald Dahl screeching and laughing into the 21st century.

THE HERALD ★ ★ ★ ★

The five Enfants are raffishly raggle-taggle in appearance and impressively slick in performance. Shadow-play and puppetry are nicely integrated into the ensemble proceedings, as is the live music which takes jolly circus oompah down into the cellar-shadows of a 1930s Berlin nightclub – and then comes up smiling in time to do a sight-gag or two. Older kids and adults with a liking for Roald Dahl will be in their element here.

THE SCOTSMAN ★ ★ ★ ★

Any show that cites Roald Dahl and Tim Burton in its publicity material has a lot to live up to. Comparing your narrative to one of the finest children's writers who ever lived and your direction to a filmmaker whose middle name is innovation is a dangerous business. But do you know, they're right. *The Terrible Infants* captures elements of both men's work – and then wraps it up in a theatricality all its own... Master of alliteration and rhyme, Lansley holds the show together with his cut-glass diction and flamboyant narration. And each story is backed by a cornucopia of instruments, played by every member of this superb cast.

THE GUARDIAN

These cautionary tales are terrific fun, poised somewhere between *Shockheaded Peter* and Roald Dahl's nastiest stories... Grownups will enjoy this trip back to the nursery, where all the cruel children have been let loose and are crying for attention... Tilly's fate is threaded through the show's wittily scripted and visually inventive 60 minutes... The pleasures and lurking perils of the nursery are conjured with some nifty shadow play, and the cast – who look like they have raided the dressing-up box and mum's makeup – are enormously versatile.

THE DAILY MIRROR ★ ★ ★ ★ ★

The use of stage props is evocative and professional throughout this faultless show. For kids or adults alike, these morality tales are simply tremendous fun and the performers are some of the best you'll see in this genre. A total delight from start to finish.

FRINGE REVIEW ★★★★★

Les Enfants Terribles' newest creation *The Terrible Infants* is an absolute delight of a show... these are new and original moral fables performed with such a sense of conviction and glee that they are just as enthralling to adults and children alike... Les Enfants Terribles are a very special company that deserves to go far – so be sure to tell your friends, family and anyone who will listen about them!... Colourful and wickedly fun this is storytelling as it should be.

HAIRLINE ★★★★★

A blend of The Brothers Grimm's fantasy, a bit of Roald Dahl's imagination and some of Tim Burton's prose and visuals... It seems Les Enfants Terribles are not scared of anything, and everything they tackle turns to gold. Missing a show by Les Enfants Terribles would normally constitute somewhat of a sacrilege, but missing *The Terrible Infants* should be penalised by law. If ever there was a more perfect little show, this is it.

The Terrible Infants was originally performed in Pleasance Two at the 2007 Edinburgh Fringe Festival. This original production did not contain the story of 'Beatrice'.

The Cast were:
NARRATOR – Oliver Lansley
MALE STORYTELLER – Matt Ian Kelly
FEMALE STORYTELLER – Nicole Lewis
MALE MUSICIAN – Tomas Gisby
MALE MUSICIAN 2 – Neil Townsend

After Edinburgh the part of MALE MUSICIAN 2 was replaced by Rachel Dawson and the role changed and developed into what is listed in this script as FEMALE MUSICIAN. The narration of BEATRICE was recorded by Dame Judi Dench.

Designer – Sam Wyer
Music – Tomas Gisby and Neil Townsend

The piece was devised by The Company with additional direction from James Seager.

ACT 1

We see a stage full of various odd shapes and objects all covered in old discoloured dust sheets. At the back of the stage is a large dressing-up style toy box. (Note. The box remains in full view of the audience throughout the whole time they are entering the auditorium.) There is also a large open storybook resting centre stage.

After a musical introduction, an old-fashioned alarm clock goes off. The lid of the box moves, then suddenly bursts open and the NARRATOR emerges (he seems far too big to fit in it). He walks towards the large storybook and picks it up cautiously and opens it. After a musical flourish he begins.

NARRATOR: Tilly loved telling tales, but the tales Tilly told tended to be totally untrue.

Little Tilly loved to lie, she didn't know why, it just made her feel funny inside,

Like the buzzing of a little bee in her belly, excited from too much honey.

He pulls off a dust sheet to reveal MALE MUSICIAN and FEMALE MUSICIAN – they have been playing the musical accompaniment. They are surrounded by many weird and wonderful looking instruments including a miniature piano.

NARRATOR: Each little lie to her was like a treat, like riding on a rollercoaster or sucking on a sugary sweet.

She never considered the cost of her corrupt concoctions.

As far as she was concerned consequences were continental cars

and repercussions were the repetitive rhythms of a big bass drum.

He pulls off another dust sheet to reveal a huge old-fashioned cart. (Note. The cart is used throughout the show in all different ways to represent many different places/things.)

NARRATOR: She'd say she had when she hadn't and she
hadn't when she had,

said she couldn't when she wouldn't, which drove
everybody mad.

*A MALE STORYTELLER and a FEMALE STORYTELLER suddenly
appear from inside the cart.*

MALE STORYTELLER: 'A Lion ate my homework.'

FEMALE STORYTELLER: 'My granny isn't well,'

MALE STORYTELLER: 'That glass of cola spilt itself, I saw the
way it fell.'

FEMALE STORYTELLER: 'I cannot go to school today the
doctor says I'm dying.'

MALE MUSICIAN: 'I saw a giant porky pig and guess what...? It
was flying!'

FEMALE STORYTELLER: He did it,

MALE STORYTELLER: She did it,

FEMALE STORYTELLER: I didn't know,

MALE STORYTELLER: I wasn't there,

FEMALE STORYTELLER: I didn't see,

MALE STORYTELLER: It couldn't be,

FEMALE STORYTELLER: It never was because,

MALE STORYTELLER: because...

FEMALE STORYTELLER: Because.

NARRATOR: She'd stuff her stories with so many staggering
slurs that she was sometimes sick from the incessant
spinning of so many yarns.

But she didn't care. She simply loved to lie.

The STORYTELLERS emerge from the cart and proceed to act out the following dialogue.

NARRATOR: One day as Tilly toddled along her merry way
manufacturing her most recent melody of miscellaneous
mistrusts.
She came across a strange old lady staggering slowly down
the street.
Hunched and stooped, her skin sagged and bagged
and wrinkled and crinkled and hung from her brittle bony
body.
Upon her back she carried a sack that begged to burst all
over the dusty dirt track.
It whimpered and whined, it grunted and groaned,
it bleated and bellyached, it mumbled and moaned
Tilly watched as the sack's seams stretched and the stitches
slowly started to snap.
Until finally with one exhausted but triumphant tear
the sack relented and liberated its load all over the road

MALE STORYTELLER: *(Playing the part of the OLD WOMAN.)*

'little girl, little girl,'

NARRATOR: crowed the old crone.

MALE STORYTELLER: 'Perhaps you could help me in picking
up this pile of my precious possessions.'

NARRATOR: Tilly looked down at the mammoth mess and
thought what long and tedious time it would take to tidy.

FEMALE STORYTELLER: *(Playing the part of TILLY.)*

'I'd love to.'

NARRATOR: chirped Tilly...

FEMALE STORYTELLER: 'but...'

NARRATOR: And the long list of lies leapt effortlessly to her mind,
Twirling around her tongue, each praying to be picked.

FEMALE STORYTELLER: 'I have a meeting with a magician
and I mustn't keep him waiting.

He's teaching me to turn cabbage into candy, quite a tasty
trick I'm sure you will agree.

So I'm awfully sorry but as you can see I simply cannot
stay to help.'

NARRATOR: The old woman looked at her as if she could see
right through her fragile flesh and bone.

MALE STORYTELLER: 'You know it's a terrible thing to tell
tales.'

NARRATOR: The old hag hissed...

Tilly paused for a moment, never having been caught out
so quickly before and resolved to carry on, she was after all
the best in the bluffing business.

FEMALE STORYTELLER: 'It's the truth!'

NARRATOR: Chirped Tilly.

But her conviction and confidence began to drain from her
brain,

As the old woman's eyes dug deeper and deeper into the
depths of her soul,

where Tilly knew there was a hole,

where the truth should have been.

MALE STORYTELLER: 'When you tell too many tall tales, those
tales have a tendency to take over,

growing bigger and uglier and stronger and scarier,

layering lie upon lie, fib upon fib.

White lies turn to grey and grey turns to black,

while you're lugging around this huge tale on your back

It's always behind you, but none of it's true,

And soon you can't control the tale, it is the tale that
controls you!'

NARRATOR: Tilly looked up at the old lady whose eyes burnt
with a fierce flame.

'Tumb and his Mum' – David G Monteith-Hodge

But rather than heed this word of warning.
She simply laughed and skipped off down the dusty dirt track,
Leaving the old lady to clean up her clutter herself.

A drum beat interrupts the story and readies us for 'Tumb'.

The character of TUMB is portrayed by a large puppet head and a series of increasingly large umbrellas to represent his increasing stomach.

NARRATOR: (*Holding up large puppet TUMB's head.*)
This is Tumb.

FEMALE STORYTELLER: (*Holding up an umbrella designed to look like TUMB's tum.*)
This is Tumb's Tum.

MALE MUSICIAN: (*Pointing at MALE STORYTELLER.*)
This is Tumb's Mum.

Beat.

This is Tumb's Mum?

MALE STORYTELLER: What? So I have to play the old woman again?

A dress and wig are thrown at him. He puts it on as the NARRATOR wolf whistles.

MALE MUSICIAN: *This* is Tumb's Mum

MALE STORYTELLER: (*As TUMB's Mum.*) Good evening.

NARRATOR: Tumb is hungry;

(*As TUMB.*) I'm Hungry!

FEMALE STORYTELLER: When Tumb is hungry his tum grunts and grumbles and groans;

(*As TUMB's Tum.*) Grrrrrrrrrrrrrrrrr

MALE STORYTELLER: Tumb's Mum says he must wait until dinner;

(*As TUMB's Mum.*) You'll wait until dinner young fellow me lad!

FEMALE STORYTELLER: Tumb's Tum says he can't wait;

(*As TUMB's Tum.*) I can't wait!

MALE STORYTELLER: Tumb's Mum says if he doesn't stop eating he will get an upset Tum;

(*As TUMB's Mum.*) If you don't stop eating you will get an upset Tum!

FEMALE STORYTELLER: Tumb's Tum disagrees;

(*As TUMB's Tum.*) I strongly disagree! Buurrp!

NARRATOR: Tumb is torn between his Tum and his Mum.

Music starts.

FEMALE STORYTELLER: (*As TUMB's Tum.*) I want sweets!

MALE MUSICIAN: Groans Tumb's Tum,

MALE STORYTELLER: (*As TUMB's Mum.*) No more sweets..

MALE MUSICIAN: Moans Tumb's Mum,

FEMALE STORYTELLER: (*As TUMB's Tum.*) I want sweets!

MALE MUSICIAN: Groans Tumb's Tum.

MALE STORYTELLER: (*As TUMB's Mum.*) No more sweets...

MALE MUSICIAN: Moans Tumb's Mum.

FEMALE STORYTELLER: (*As TUMB's Tum.*) I want sweets!

MALE STORYTELLER: (*As TUMB's Mum.*) No more sweets...

FEMALE STORYTELLER: (*As TUMB's Tum.*) I want sweets!

MALE STORYTELLER: (*As TUMB's Mum.*) NO MORE SWEETSSS!!!

FEMALE MUSICIAN: Just give him some bloomin' sweets!

FEMALE STORYTELLER and MALE MUSICIAN now feed the head of TUMB various foodstuffs provided by MALE STORYTELLER as TUMB's Mum as TUMB proceeds to get fatter and fatter.

FEMALE STORYTELLER: Tumb eats ice cream.

MALE MUSICIAN: Tumb eats cupcakes.

FEMALE STORYTELLER: Tumb eats lollies.

MALE MUSICIAN: Tumb eats busicuits.

FEMALE STORYTELLER: Tumb eats Marlon Brando!

Silence.

MALE MUSICIAN: Tumb eats bon bons.

Tumb eats... Tumb eats...

There is no food left.

FEMALE STORYTELLER: (*As TUMB's giant Tum.*) I want sweets!

MALE STORYTELLER: (*As TUMB's Mum.*) No more sweets.

FEMALE STORYTELLER: (*As TUMB's giant Tum.*) I want sweets!

MALE STORYTELLER: (*As TUMB's Mum.*) No more sweets.

FEMALE STORYTELLER: (*As TUMB's giant Tum.*) I want sweets!

MALE STORYTELLER: (*As TUMB's Mum.*) NO MORE SWEETSSS!!!

NARRATOR: Tumb is torn between his tum and his mum.

Beat.

Tumb eats his Mum!

MALE STORYTELLER: (*As TUMB's Mum.*)
Aaaaaaaaaaarrrrrrrrrrrrrgggggghhhhhhhh

Blackout.

FEMALE STORYTELLER: Now Tumb has eaten his Mum there is no one left to cook for Tumb.

Tumb's Tum begins to mutter, mumble and moan,

But something is different.

MALE STORYTELLER: (*As TUMB's Mum.*) No more sweets...

A light is turned on behind the giant umbrella now representing TUMB's Tum to reveal the silhouette of TUMB's Mum.

FEMALE STORYTELLER: ...Comes the voice from Tumb's Tum,

It's the voice of Tumb's Mum and she sounds upset.

MALE STORYTELLER: (*As TUMB's Mum.*) No more sweets!

FEMALE STORYTELLER: She mumbles, grumbles and moans.

Now Tumb has an upset Tum and an upset Mum,

NARRATOR: (*As TUMB.*) And no one left to cook for Tumb!

FEMALE STORYTELLER: As time passes Tumb's Tum begins to shrink and shrivel,

as Tumb's mum refuses to let in any more food.

Soon Tumb has almost no Tum at all and he is as thin as a stick, as skinny as a rake,

except for the Mum shaped bump that sits where his Tum used to be.

MALE STORYTELLER: (*As TUMB's Mum.*) No more sweets!

The huge umbrella has gradually been taken down as TUMB gets skinnier and skinnier.

FEMALE STORYTELLER: There will be no more sweets for Tumb.

NARRATOR: If only Tumb had listened to the moans of his Mum and not the groans of his Tum,

Maybe Tumb's Mum would still be around to cook for Tumb.

But alas all that's left is Tumb...

MALE STORYTELLER: ...and his tum shaped Mum or his Mum shaped tum...

NARRATOR: either way, there will be no more sweets for Tumb.

MALE STORYTELLER: So if you're ever torn between a moan and a groan,

listen to your Mum and not your Tum!

Music ends for TUMB and the signature tune for TILLY starts up again as the NARRATOR picks up his storybook to continue the story.

NARRATOR: Many weeks passed and Tilly continued to spout her silly stories,

uttering untold untruths and fountains of fibs, fictions and falsehoods

at every opportunity she got.

Never once deviating from her deceitful and duplicitous disposition.

Until one day Tilly did something terrible.

So terrible I'm scared to even say it out loud.

So naughty she knew she'd be in big trouble if she was ever found out.

Worse than the time she forgot to pay for those penny sweets.

Worse than the time she shattered Mother's ming vase.

Even worse than the time she tried to test if the cat really did have nine lives.

It was truly terrible and she knew that there was only one way out...

To lie like she'd never lied before,

To weave a web of deceit so grand that even the smartest spider would have been impressed by its silky strands.

And so she began...

The following sequence is told physically between the NARRATOR and FEMALE STORYTELLER. Attributing physical gestures to every character and action involved. Both acting in exact unison with one another.

FEMALE STORYTELLER: (*As TILLY.*) 'It wasn't me, it couldn't have been me,

you see, at the time the dastardly deed was done I had gone to the bakers to buy buns.

But the baker had been trapped in his oven by a wicked witch,

who'd wanted him to bake her a big gingerbread house. When he refused she bashed him on the bonce with her broom,

and bundled him into the oven!

I tried to open the oven door but it was too heavy and I simply wasn't strong enough.

NARRATOR: So I sprinted down to the woodcutters cabin, hoping he could help.

But when I reached the cutter's cottage, the cutter wasn't there.

Just a wolf, sitting at his table, smiling with satisfaction and licking his lips,

and from the beast's belly I could hear the cutter's concerned cries!

FEMALE STORYTELLER: So I ran and I ran to the butcher's in the hope he could bring his big butcher's knife...

NARRATOR: ...and rescue the woodcutter from the wolf, so the woodcutter could rescue the baker from burning in his big baker's oven.

FEMALE STORYTELLER: But when I got to the butcher's, his abode was abandoned and in the back garden was a big beanstalk...

NARRATOR: ...that carried on up into the clouds. So I scrambled up the sizeable stalk where I found a colossal castle.

FEMALE STORYTELLER: And in the castle lived a grumpy giant who had butcher-napped the butcher, with the grand plan of grinding his bones to bake his bread!

NARRATOR: I knew I had to rescue the butcher from the big bread making giant,

so the butcher could rescue the woodcutter from the wolf,
and the woodcutter could rescue the baker from burning in his big baker's oven!

FEMALE STORYTELLER: So I found the cage in which the ogre held his hostage,

and passing a golden goose along the way...

NARRATOR: ...I snuck silently past the sleeping giant, and creeping quietly, I acquired the key for the cage from the captor's clutches.

So I rescued the butcher from the big bread making giant...

FEMALE STORYTELLER: ...and we shot down the stalk and into his shop to fetch his big butcher's knife,

then scuttled to the cutter's cabin...

NARRATOR: ...where the butcher rescued the woodcutter from the wolf.

Once that was done we dashed to the baker's...

FEMALE STORYTELLER: ...where the woodcutter used his big axe to break down the door,

and rescue the baker from burning in his big baker's oven.

NARRATOR: And once everyone was rescued,

we went back to the butchers where the woodcutter hacked down the beanstalk with his hatchet...

FEMALE STORYTELLER: ...the butcher sliced up the wolf into fillets...

NARRATOR: ...and the baker baked it in a pie...

FEMALE STORYTELLER: ...which we all ate for supper.

So you see it simply couldn't have been me...

NARRATOR: ...for I was busy all day long.

MALE STORYTELLER: (*Holding the storybook.*)

Initially everyone seemed satisfied with this extraordinary explanation.

But as Tilly told this tallest of tales something very strange began to happen.

At the bottom of her back, just above her bum,

she began to feel a bizarre bump that hadn't been there before.

And as her tale got bigger and bigger, so did the bump.

Until Tilly had what could only be described as a tail attached to her tiny behind.

And as her tale grew and grew so did her tail,

snaking down her trouser leg until it poked out proudly at the bottom.

The NARRATOR is unhappy with the MALE STORYTELLER now telling the story and so grabs the book off him and continues.

NARRATOR: At first Tilly tried to hide her tail,

she'd wrap it round her waist, or strap it to her thigh,

but it simply kept escaping...

The PLAYERS have congregated around the piano and are talking loudly and conspiratorially with each other. They stop as they see the NARRATOR looking at them.

NARRATOR: (*Beginning again.*) At first Tilly tried to hide her tail,

she'd wrap it round her waist, or strap it to her thigh,

but it simply kept escaping no matter how hard she would try...

Again he is interrupted by the actions of the PLAYERS. Except this time they are just behind him. They act as if nothing is happening.

NARRATOR: (*Beginning again.*) At first Tilly tried to hide her tail,

she'd wrap it round her waist, or strap it to her thigh,

but it simply kept escaping no matter how hard she would try...

The PLAYERS produce what they were hiding behind their backs – a dustbin – and throw it over the NARRATOR's head to start the next story.

FEMALE STORYTELLER: (*Pointing at the NARRATOR with a bin over his head.*) This is Mingus!

NARRATOR: No!

MALE STORYTELLER: This is Mingus!

NARRATOR: No!

MALE STORYTELLER: This is Mingus?

NARRATOR: No!

They take the bin off, the NARRATOR is furious, he gathers himself and starts again.

NARRATOR: At first Tilly tried to hide her tail,
she'd wrap it round her waist, or strap it to her thigh,
but it simply kept escaping...

The PLAYERS push the NARRATOR back into the bin so he is sitting in it and is now stuck. They are free to start the next story referring to the NARRATOR now as the character of MINGUS.

FEMALE STORYTELLER: This is Mingus!

MALE STORYTELLER: Mingus is filthy!

FEMALE STORYTELLER: Mingus is so filthy in fact that fungus grows from Mingus,

GRUMPY: Or did Mingus grow from fungus?

FEMALE STORYTELLER: No one could quite remember.

MALE STORYTELLER & FEMALE STORYTELLER: Whatever Mingus' fingers fiddle with becomes riddled with filth and fungus!

MALE STORYTELLER: Wherever he puts his mitts goes mouldy.

FEMALE STORYTELLER: Whatever he touches turns to toadstools.

MALE STORYTELLER: Wherever he stands stinks and stagnates.

FEMALE STORYTELLER: Mingus Mings!

MALE STORYTELLER & FEMALE STORYTELLER: Mingus Mings.
Mingus Mings.
Mingus MINGS!!!!

MINGUS drags himself off stage dejected.

MALE MUSICIAN: No one wanted to play with Mingus...

FEMALE STORYTELLER: because they don't want to start growing fungus!

MALE STORYTELLER: And besides not many can stand the stench, the whiff, the honk, the hummm,
That seems to follow Mingus,

FEMALE STORYTELLER: Or that Mingus seems to follow.

Pause – there is a drumroll as the PLAYERS introduce MINGUS.

MALE STORYTELLER: He's dirtier than dirt,

FEMALE STORYTELLER: He's grimier than grime.

MALE STORYTELLER: He'd be doing time, if being mucky was a crime.

MALE STORYTELLER & FEMALE STORYTELLER: Here's Mingus...

The NARRATOR emerges from behind the cart with the bin on his bottom and wearing the MINGUS mask. The mask sits on top of his head and he bends over to show the face, giving MINGUS a

43

slightly distorted physicality. He acts out the following story with the PLAYERS.

MALE STORYTELLER: Mingus tried to have a bath once,

FEMALE STORYTELLER: but he was so grubby that he turned the water into slime.

MALE STORYTELLER: And what used to be his bathtub is now a stinky swamp,

FEMALE STORYTELLER: swimming with smelly creatures,

MALE STORYTELLER: many species still unknown to science,

FEMALE STORYTELLER: But impossible to investigate,

MALE STORYTELLER: as it is too infested for scientists to explore.

MALE MUSICIAN: (*Trying to join in on the banter.*)
Yeah, yeah, yeah I hear they are working on a new stink-proof suit but as yet nothing can withstand the ming of Mingus...

Silence.

...Because he smells?

FEMALE MUSICIAN: At school... (*She coughs, and the PLAYERS all run into school positions, sitting cross-legged.*) At school
Mingus has to sit in the middle of a nearby field,
And watch the teacher through a telescope.
So as not to put off his fellow pupils...

FEMALE STORYTELLER & MALE STORYTELLER: ...with his putrid pong!

MALE MUSICIAN: Sometimes Mingus gets miserable,
because even the flies won't follow him around,
finding him too grotty even by their stinking standards.
Mingus doesn't really want to be manky,
But then he doesn't really want to wash either.

MALE STORYTELLER: Mingus' home is so full of mess and muck,

that there is no longer any room for Mingus,

And he has to sleep outside in the dustbin to keep warm.

FEMALE MUSICIAN: One rare day, when the bin men made a brave visit to his house,

they picked up Mingus' Bin (which still had Mingus in),

And chucked it in the back of their big bin van.

Poor little Mingus was still fast asleep,

Snoring soundly as the truck sped away.

MINGUS is carted away.

NARRATOR: (*As himself.*)

And so that was the last that anyone ever saw of little Mingus,

Though not the last they saw of fungus.

Some say he is now dwelling at the dump,

where he feels quite at home. So...

MALE STORYTELLER: (*Interrupting him by putting the bin over his head.*)

...if you encounter Mingus,

be sure to wash your fingers...

FEMALE STORYTELLER: Or you may just find that fungus starts to grow all over you!

The NARRATOR walks off with the bin over his head. The PLAYERS then clear up and disappear. The NARRATOR removes the bin and tentatively returns. He looks around for the book and when he finds it, attempts to carry on with the story of TILLY.

NARRATOR: At first Tilly tried to hide her tail.

She'd wrap it round her waist, or strap it to her thigh...

FEMALE STORYTELLER interrupts him by making the buzzing noise of a bee. The STORYTELLER becomes distracted by the 'bee'. Before trying to continue.

'Mingus' – David G Monteith-Hodge

NARRATOR: At first Tilly tried to hide her tail...

FEMALE STORYTELLER: Buzzzzzzzzzz

Pause.

NARRATOR: At first Tilly...

FEMALE STORYTELLER: Buzzzzzzzzz

NARRATOR: At first Tilly...

FEMALE STORYTELLER: Buzzzzzzzzz

The NARRATOR slams the book shut, squashing the 'bee'. He then re-opens the book and the bee buzzes feebly to the ground. The NARRATOR grins and continues.

NARRATOR: At first Tilly tried to hide her tail...

FEMALE STORYTELLER: BUZZZZZZZZZZZZZZ!!

NARRATOR: Oh for goodness sake!

Blackout.

FEMALE MUSICIAN emerges and pulls out an old vinyl record placing it on what appears to be an old gramophone. The remaining story is played out as a Voiceover whilst the PLAYERS act out the story in a dumb show.

VOICEOVER: Beatrice had a bee in her bonnet.
   She loved to talk but loathed to listen.
   Stuck in her own little world she'd talk and talk and talk;
   Jibber jabber, yakkety yak, blabbery blather, chittery chat.
   Bea cared very little for what others had to say,
   Let's put it this way;
   She'd be a mastermind if her specialist subject were herself.
   She was so full of hot air she could fill a balloon and fly it
   to the moon and back without being out of breath.
   She talked so much that all the donkeys in the village
   where she lived were missing hind-legs.
   She'd just go on and on and on and on.

A sheet is held up from behind which the silhouette of BEATRICE appears, chatting away.

'Did I ever tell you about when I did this, that and the other?
I know him and I know her, I've met his sister and his brother.
Did you hear about the time that I went there back again?
Did I mention who and what and why and how and where and when?
I, I, I,
Me, me, me,
My, my, my,
Bea, Bea, Bea!'

The sheet is dropped down to reveal the BEATRICE puppet in place of the human silhouette.

VOICEOVER: That was all she cared about.
So much so that sometimes she barely noticed the other people around her.
In fact, as far as she was concerned, other people were only there so that she could talk to them about herself.
She simply loved the sound of her own voice.

FEMALE MUSICIAN plays a violin to represent BEATRICE's voice.

VOICEOVER: She'd listen to it all day if she was given a choice.
Natter, chatter, babble, gabble, blah blah blah blah, bzzzzzzzzzz...
She talked so much that her voice had begun to take on a rather extraordinary tone,
It was sort of a hum, like a buzz, or a drone.
The pitch was peculiar, a very strange sound,
Like a bevy of bees, her words buzzing around.

One sunny summer's day as Beatrice was busy banging on about one thing or another.
A hard-working honeybee was hovering by...

The NARRATOR appears holding a bee, he makes a bee noise with a kazoo. The bee slowly becomes entranced by BEATRICE.

VOICEOVER: ...when it became seduced by a strange hypnotic hum.

'I, I, I

Me, me, me

My, my, my

Bea, Bea, Beazzzzzzzzzzzzzzzzzzzzzzzz'

Bee noise.

VOICEOVER: Unbeknown to Beatrice the bee had become bewitched by this bizarre buzzing...

Bee noise.

VOICEOVER: ...Mesmerised by its musical murmur...

Bee noise.

VOICEOVER: ...And without thinking the buzzing bumble zoomed straight into Beatrice's Beehive hairdo...

The bee flies into BEATRICE's hair.

VOICEOVER: ...Where it started to make itself at home.

Bee noise.

VOICEOVER: At first Beatrice barely noticed the delicate drone coming from her lovely locks,

And she continued to blather and blab and gossip and gas.

But the humming inside her haircut was getting louder every day,

And as each line of language left her lips,

Another brainwashed bumblebee would buzz into her barnet.

The NARRATOR pulls out one bee, then another.

MALE STORYTELLER, followed by the MALE MUSICIAN join the NARRATOR with more bees.

VOICEOVER: Like a pied piper, playing magical music,
    Bea's dulcet drones entranced the intoxicated insects.
    Bees would fly from miles around,
    Attracted by this magical sound,
    'til Bea had bees from everywhere,
    Now nesting in her beehive hair.

The bees all hover around BEATRICE's head.

VOICEOVER: Soon people started to avoid Beatrice,
    Even more than usual.
    Scared stiff of the stinging storm-cloud that swarmed
    around her.
    But Bea was wrapped up so tightly in herself that she
    barely noticed.
    She had become almost oblivious to the existence of
    others.
    When she approached, people would run in the opposite
    direction,
    But all this meant was that she'd have to talk even louder
    to be heard.
    And now she shouted every word.

    'I, I, I
    ME, ME, ME
    MY, MY, MY
    BEA, BEA, BEAZZZZZZZZZZZZZZZZZZZ'

And the louder she got and the more noise she made,
The more bees would arrive, zooming into the hive.

*NARRATOR, MALE STORYTELLER and MALE MUSICIAN emerge now
with hundreds of bees that fly all over the stage and the audience.
Building to a musical crescendo.*

VOICEOVER: Until one day Beatrice awoke to find herself in
    the dark.

*FEMALE MUSICIAN emerges as BEATRICE now with a huge beehive
puppet mask head on.*

VOICEOVER: The billions of busy bees had built a big beehive right around Beatrice's bonce.

And now you could hardly even see her head,

Just the top of her hair, poking out at the hive's highest point.

Beatrice bumbled around in the blackness, bumping, banging and bashing into everything.

'Blooming Beeeessszzzzzzzzzzzzzzzzzzz!'

She cried out but no one could hear her through the thick walls of the hive.

And so for the first time that anyone could remember Bea was speechless.

Poor Bea unable to see or to speak.

And stuck with nothing but honey to eat.

Everyone was a little taken aback by the new Beatrice.

Though many actually preferred her this way,

as for the first ever time she had nothing to say.

'Don't just zzzzzzstand there you zzzzzzzzzzzzzzstinking nincompoopsssssszzzzzzzzzz help meeeeee!'

She would scream... but all they could hear was a gentle...

The violin again represents BEATRICE's voice. As she 'speaks' the PLAYERS then join in with other instruments. A small section of music is played before the PLAYERS exit, leaving BEATRICE alone.

VOICEOVER: At first Beatrice was understandably upset by this unpleasant predicament.

Not so much the bees in her hair or the hive on her head,

But more the fact that no one could hear what she said.

She hated not being heard, not being able to jibber jabber or yakkety yak,

blabbery blather and chittery chat,

Natter, chatter, babble, gabble,

burble and blab, gossip and gas.

She wanted to talk about me, me, me, me!

And so she decided to talk to the bees.

Two of the PLAYERS return with bees to 'talk' to BEATRICE. They mirror her violin sounds with their kazoos.

VOICE OVER: And before long she'd appointed herself as Queen Bee.

Buzzing, blabbing, babbling and blathering more than ever before.

The next section is illustrated with shadow play behind the sheet once more.

VOICE OVER: Beatrice was in seventh heaven.

Surrounded by a swarm of loyal subjects, hanging off her every word.

However, the locals were less enamoured by Queen Bea.

They simply couldn't cope with the cloud of creepy critters that were trespassing in their town.

These bees were a bother, a bellyache and a burden.

A plague of pests polluting picnics and breaking up barbecues.

People couldn't even go outside any longer, for fear of falling foul of this fearsome foe.

Buzzing and zipping and whizzing and stinging.

They were a menace, a nuisance.

And so, they simply had to go.

And Beatrice was banished.

Brian, the local brave beekeeper, bedecked in full protective paraphernalia,

took Beatrice by the hand and led her out into the forest on the far reaches of town where she was left to fend for herself.

BEATRICE is taken into the forest.

VOICEOVER: At first Beatrice didn't even really notice the lack
of company.

She never really paid that much attention to the people
around her anyway.

She was quite content with her brigade of bees to blab
away to.

But as the weeks wandered by, even the bees began to get
bored.

Sick of hearing about:

'I, I, I
Me, me, me
My, my, my
Bea, Bea, Beazzzzzzzzzzzzzzzzzzzzzzzzzz'

And eventually, unable to bear her bottomless banter,
They abandoned their beehive and just buzzed off.

And so she was all alone.

Stuck in a forest with a head-full of honey and not a friend
in the world.

But once again, wrapped up tightly within her own little
mind,

She just kept on nattering, chattering, babbling and
gabbling.

And so she barely even noticed the absence of the bees.

Jibber jabber, yakkety yak, blabbery blather, chittery chat,
Natter, chatter, babble, gabble,
burble and blab, gossip and gas.

And as she filled the forest with all her hot air,
the buzzing caught the attentions of a great grizzly bear.

*A euphonium (or similar) is played to represent the growling of a
bear. The other PLAYERS hold a giant bear puppet ominously over
BEATRICE. She continues to 'talk' with her violin.*

VOICEOVER: Stirred from its slumber by her yummy honey's scent.

Bear sound – euphonium.

VOICEOVER: The great big bear wandered through the woods towards Bea's hypnotic humming,
And if she'd only known how to listen she might have heard it coming.

Bear sound – euphonium.

VOICEOVER: But she sat there wittering and chittering and chattering and nattering,
until she felt a gentle hand rest upon her shoulder.

Bear sound – euphonium.

VOICEOVER: Suddenly Bea's heart filled with excitement.
Someone to talk to, she'd found herself a friend,
She finally had another brand-new ear which she could bend.
But unable to see, she wasn't aware,
That her new companion was a grizzly bear.
The bear let out a growl that would fill most people with dread.

Bear sound – euphonium.

VOICEOVER: But Bea didn't listen she just talked instead.

'I, I, I
Me, me, me
My, my, my
Bea, Bea, Beazzzzzzzzzzzzzzzzzzzzzzzzz'

She reached up to the huge hand upon her shoulder;

'My what big gloveszzzzz you're wearing, I used to have a pair of gloveszzzzz just like that.'

The bear let out another grim, grizzly growl.

Bear sound – euphonium.

VOICEOVER: But Beatrice didn't listen, she was too busy
boring him with her own blathery blab.

'My what a lovely thick coat you have, is it bearzzzzzzskin?
I bet it's very comfortable, but not aszzzz comfortable
aszzzzz my coat.'

Bear sound – euphonium.

'My what a big szzzzzzzzzzzmile you have, all those big
teeth, I have perfect teeth...'

Bear sound – euphonium.

'Oh Gosh, what bad breath you have, I can barely bear it'

*The euphonium and music build to a crescendo as the giant bear
head puppet gets closer and closer to BEATRICE with its mouth wide
open. It suddenly slams shut.*

Blackout.

VOICEOVER: Now as for what happened next it's really quite
hard to say.
Some reckon that the bees came back and scared the bear
away.
Others think that Beatrice bored the bear into a trance.
Or perhaps the Bear and Bea made friends and moved
away to France.
There's just one universal fact upon which everyone
agrees,
And that is 'bears like honey but they don't like bees.'

Interval.

'Beatrice and her Bees' – David G Monteith-Hodge

ACT TWO

The PLAYERS all enter with instruments and play the tune 'Bananas'. Eventually they all finish one by one until the NARRATOR is still playing on his own. The others gather round the storybook, eventually the NARRATOR realises and stops; slightly embarrassed, he then rushes to join the others for the story.

FEMALE STORYTELLER: At first Tilly tried to hide her tail.

The NARRATOR is unimpressed and grabs the book back to tell the tale himself.

NARRATOR: At first Tilly tried to hide her tail.
She'd wrap it round her waist, or strap it to her thigh,
But it simply kept escaping no matter how hard she would try.
And she was forced to start telling more tales to keep it under wraps
But with every tale her tail grew bigger and stronger and longer and longer and longer and longer, and soon it started making mischief all by itself!
As Tilly slept, her tail would sneak off and snake off down the street...

The other PLAYERS 'snake' off around the stage as the MALE MUSICIAN plays an alto sax (or similar) to represent the tale.

FEMALE STORYTELLER: Poking policeman,

MALE STORYTELLER: Upsetting apple carts,

FEMALE STORYTELLER: Toppling toddlers,

MALE STORYTELLER: Bothering barmaids,

FEMALE STORYTELLER: Scaring school children,

MALE STORYTELLER: And harassing hairdressers.

NARRATOR: The townspeople started asking questions as to who was behind these dastardly deeds.

FEMALE STORYTELLER: And sadly for poor Tilly it was to her whom all the tale's terrible trails would lead.

NARRATOR: Tilly told even taller tales to try and get herself off the hook.

MALE STORYTELLER: But once again with every appalling untruth she told,
her tail would grow and grow and grow.

NARRATOR: Until one day Tilly's trousers couldn't take it anymore.
The seams stretched and the stitches slowly started to snap, until finally with one exhausted but triumphant tear they ripped...!

A huge tail appears, created by the PLAYERS.

NARRATOR: And out burst this huge thick black glossy tail, that was almost as big as Tilly herself.
People were shocked and looked at Tilly with surprise.
What was this monstrous appendage that they saw before their eyes?
They began to get suspicious and question what was true,
And soon they remembered that terrible thing she'd sworn she didn't do.
So terrible I'm scared to even say it out loud.

FEMALE STORYTELLER: Worse than when she cheated on her English examination.

MALE STORYTELLER: Worse than when she replaced Mummy's medicine with sweeties.

MALE MUSICIAN: Even worse than when she tried to put her bunny in the oven.

FEMALE STORYTELLER: That night Tilly went to bed burning with a fear of being found out,

What if they spoke to the baker?

MALE STORYTELLER: Or the woodcutter?

MALE MUSICIAN: Or the butcher?

FEMALE STORYTELLER: If they did they were sure to find out she was fibbing and they would know the terrible truth!

NARRATOR: But it wasn't just Tilly who was troubled.
Tilly's tail was terrified, fearing for its very existence,
And so it decided to take matters into its own hands.

The other PLAYERS slam the book shut and take it away from the NARRATOR.

Music fades and lights dim for the next story. MALE MUSICIAN sings 'Thingummyboy' as the story is told by the NARRATOR and FEMALE STORYTELLER. MALE STORYTELLER operates the puppet of THINGUMMYBOY.

The story is told through a mixture of slides and shadow puppetry which interact with the THINGUMMYBOY puppet.

MALE MUSICIAN: (*Singing.*)
Out of sight out of mind like toys left on the shelf,
A clever chameleon, disguising himself,
Never leaving an impression, a stain or a mark,
He was perfectly happy to sit in the dark.
Out of sight, out of view, he was never quite there,
Nobody knew him but he just didn't care.
'Where's Thingummyboy?' the people would say,
Then forget who he was and just be on their way.

NARRATOR: Did I ever tell you about Whodgimaflip? Oh whatsisname?
You know Thingummyboy?
He looks kind of... like well – sort of... – he's quite hard to place.
I'm sorry to say I've forgotten his face.

You see the thing about Thingummyboy is that he was so
terribly shy.
He thought no one would listen, so he just didn't try.
So bland he could blend into backgrounds at will,
It was quite a skill, keeping that still.
Keeping out of the way, never saying a word,
Thingummyboy was not seen AND not heard.

MALE MUSICIAN: (*Singing.*)
Out of sight out of mind like toys left on the shelf,
A clever chameleon, camouflaging himself,
Never leaving an impression, a stain or a mark,
He was perfectly happy to sit in the dark.
Out of sight, out of view, he was never quite there,
Nobody knew him but he just didn't care,
'Where's Thingummyboy?' the people would say,
Then forget who he was and just be on their way.

FEMALE STORYTELLER: One fateful day things turned for the
worse.
What he thought was a blessing was becoming a curse.
It started at school with the register list,
When suddenly one day his name was just missed.
He tried to speak out, to make a complaint,
But nobody heard him, his voice was too faint.
So he hid in the cupboard and kept out of the way,
And then left at the end of the day.

MALE MUSICIAN: (*Singing.*)
Out of sight, out of reach, he was never around,
Perfectly practiced, not making a sound,
Never leaving an impression, a stain or a mark,
He was perfectly happy to sit in the dark.
Out of sight, out of view, he was never quite there,
Nobody knew him but he just didn't care,
'Where's Thingummyboy?' the people would say,
Then forget who he was and just be on their way.

FEMALE STORYTELLER: Frightfully forgettable.

NARRATOR: Remarkably unremarkable.

FEMALE STORYTELLER: Miraculously unmemorable.

NARRATOR: Poor Thingummyboy.
    He stood at the bus stop but the bus just drove by.
    The driver didn't see him, he didn't know why.
    Not that he minded, but the walk was quite long,
    And he couldn't help feeling that something was wrong.
    When he got home for dinner, it was getting quite late.
    He sat at the table awaiting his plate.
    He sat there for hours but the table stayed bare.
    It was almost as if he just wasn't there.

Musical Interlude.

FEMALE STORYTELLER: So he climbed up the stairs, to get
    ready for bed.
    With a grumbling stomach, and an ache in his head.
    But it seems in his absence his mother decided
    to redecorate the room in which he resided.
    Poor Thingummyboy's heart soon filled up with gloom,
    Upon realising his bedroom was now a spare room.
    He nearly said something but thought it was best
    To continue his silent protest.
    Poor Thingummyboy curled on the floor,
    No blanket, no pillow and a draught from the door.
    He wanted to scream and wake up the whole house.
    But instead he just lay there as quiet as a mouse.

    *NARRATOR and MALE MUSICIAN join in singing the words alongside
    the FEMALE STORYTELLER speaking them.*

FEMALE STORYTELLER: The next morning he woke at the
    cracking of dawn.
    As stiff as can be, he let out a huge yawn,
    And headed to the bathroom for his morning routine,

To have a quick wash and give his teeth a good clean.
He rolled up his sleeves and pulled down his hood,
Gazed in the mirror but things didn't look good.
He stared at the spot where his face should have been,
But he saw no reflection, no face, to be seen.
Even the mirror had forgotten his face.

NARRATOR: And in place of that face was simply a space.

FEMALE STORYTELLER: In horror he gasped, and tried to cry out...

NARRATOR: ...But his voice had forgotten to shout.

MALE STORYTELLER: Now this is what happened and I know it sounds weird,
But Thingummyboy had simply disappeared.
He'd become so adept at not being missed,
Poor Thingummyboy now ceased to exist.
And so sadly it ends,
Out of sight and out of mind,
Thingummyboy left his whole life behind.
So if you think you've seen a ghost or feel something in the air,
It could be poor Thingummyboy, trying to let you know he's there.

*The music comes to an end and the stage is set for the next story –
'Linena'.*

*The NARRATOR grabs the book and attempts to restart 'Tilly' but is
interrupted by coloured cloths flying out of the cart. He attempts to
investigate but is showered with hundreds of different coloured cloths
flying everywhere. The music for LINENA starts, and the LINENA
puppet emerges.*

NARRATOR: Little Linena was made of cloth.
And wherever she went little bits got torn off.
So she had to replace them with pieces she picked up,
From tailors and retailers and second-hand shops.

Now each part of little Linena was a patch,
Though none of them matched.
Her toes were old towels,

FEMALE STORYTELLER: Her legs were linen.

MALE STORYTELLER: Her hips were hessian.

FEMALE STORYTELLER: Her stomach, a sack...

NARRATOR: ...and so was her back.

MALE STORYTELLER: Her chest, cheap polyester.

FEMALE STORYTELLER: Her shoulders shabby suede.

MALE MUSICIAN: Her arms were another unpleasant artificial fibre, leading to her used handkerchief hands.

FEMALE STORYTELLER: Her neck an old knitted cardy.

MALE STORYTELLER: Her face a filthy flannel.

NARRATOR: And her long, lank hair, the laces of a hundred old boots.
But little Linena was sad.
She didn't like being patchy...

MALE STORYTELLER: a hotchpotch,

FEMALE STORYTELLER: a mishmash,

NARRATOR: She longed to be made of finer fabric.

MALE STORYTELLER: To be at the forefront of fashion, like all those famous faces she sees on the covers of magazines,
Flouncing around on the catwalks,

FEMALE STORYTELLER: She coveted quality and ached to be expensive.
To be made of material so soft that it demands to be touched and stroked.

NARRATOR: And so one day little Linena stole some scissors
And off she went snip snip, snip snip.

NARRATOR, MALE STORYTELLER & FEMALE STORYTELLER:
Cutting and slashing and tearing and hacking, ripping and chopping.
Snip snip, snip snip.
Sneaking and stealing and grabbing and thieving, a bit here, a bit there.
Snip snip, snip snip.

NARRATOR: A wealthy old widow, taking tea in Chelsea with her little Chihuahuas...

NARRATOR, MALE STORYTELLER & FEMALE STORYTELLER:
Snip snip, snip snip.

NARRATOR: A young royal at the races, trussed up to the nines...

NARRATOR, MALE STORYTELLER & FEMALE STORYTELLER:
Snip snip, snip snip.

FEMALE STORYTELLER: An alluring actress at a premiere, dressed for the press...

NARRATOR, MALE STORYTELLER & FEMALE STORYTELLER:
Snip snip, snip snip.

FEMALE STORYTELLER: A famous fashionista, flashing flesh for photographers...

'Snip, snip' – David G Monteith-Hodge

NARRATOR, MALE STORYTELLER & FEMALE STORYTELLER: Snip snip, snip snip.

NARRATOR: And now little Linena had more marvellous material than she could ever have dreamed of, so, she started to sew...

LINENA goes into the cart and we hear 'making stuff' sounds.

NARRATOR: And soon...

LINENA re-emerges – a totally new puppet, now all glossy and made from beautiful, expensive materials.

MALE STORYTELLER: She had fabulous feet of the finest fur, With tweed toes...

FEMALE STORYTELLER: ...And legs of luscious leather. Her hips were now of the highest quality.

MALE STORYTELLER: Her stomach spun from the smoothest and snuggest sheep's wool.

FEMALE STORYTELLER: Her chest chiffon.

MALE STORYTELLER: Her shoulders silk.

FEMALE STORYTELLER: Her arms angora, with fashionable fabric fingers on handsome hand-knitted hands.

MALE STORYTELLER: Her neck was now quality cashmere, And her face was the most fabulous feature of all, Made from voluptuous velvet with Chihuahua fur cheeks.

FEMALE STORYTELLER: And her long hair was no longer bootlaces but braided from the wool of Tibetan llamas.

MALE MUSICIAN: Linena looked lovely, and she was very proud.

NARRATOR: So proud she freely flounced up and down the streets to show off her new threads...

LINENA moves to the front of the stage and performs a routine. The MALE MUSICIAN plays the saxophone which acts as her voice as she sings in front of her adoring public.

NARRATOR: And just as she wished she was now so soft and special,

That strangers in the street would stop her,

FEMALE STORYTELLER: and stroke her,

MALE MUSICIAN: and prod her,

MALE STORYTELLER: and poke her,

NARRATOR: and pat her,

FEMALE STORYTELLER: and push her,

MALE STORYTELLER: and grab her,

FEMALE STORYTELLER: and grope her.

MALE STORYTELLER: and soon all those grimy, grubby fingers began to take their toll...

FEMALE STORYTELLER: ...and little Linena's lovely looks were all sullied and soiled,

And tatty and torn.

FEMALE MUSICIAN: But when she tried to wash herself inside her washing machine...

The PLAYERS act out putting LINENA into a washing machine – the spinning of the cartwheel acts as the washing machine.

FEMALE MUSICIAN: Disaster struck! As all her different parts were either handwash or dry-clean.

The old, tatty LINENA re-emerges.

NARRATOR: And so she was ruined and ragged once more.
Poor little Linena all patchy and mis-matchy.
And to top it all she was set upon by furious followers of fashion,

Enraged by the chunks that had been cheekily chopped
from their favourite glamorous garments.

They brandished their scissors with violent vengeance.

The wild old widow, with her howling, hairless hounds...

NARRATOR, MALE STORYTELLER & FEMALE STORYTELLER:
Snip snip, snip snip.

FEMALE STORYTELLER: The extremely angry actress pursued
by paparazzi...

NARRATOR, MALE STORYTELLER & FEMALE STORYTELLER:
Snip snip, snip snip.

MALE STORYTELLER: The furious fashionista, fuming at the
hole in her otherwise flawless frock...

NARRATOR, MALE STORYTELLER & FEMALE STORYTELLER:
Snip snip, snip snip.

NARRATOR: The really rather irate royal on returning from
the races...

NARRATOR, MALE STORYTELLER & FEMALE STORYTELLER:
Snip snip, snip snip, snip snip, snip snip, snip snip,
snip snip, snip snip, snip snip...

MALE MUSICIAN: And once the snips finally stopped,
There was very little left of Linena.

FEMALE MUSICIAN: Just a few rags and threads and scraps,
hardly enough for a little girl at all.

NARRATOR: There are many moral lessons to be learnt from
poor little Linena,

I'm sure you won't have missed them all.

But spare a thought for her, the next time you wash your
socks.

It's not easy being a material girl.

*The story and music ends. The NARRATOR looks for the storybook
but the FEMALE STORYTELLER now has it. She storms over and
pushes it into his hand, forcing him to finish the story.*

NARRATOR: Late that night when everyone was asleep, and it was as dark as dark could be,

Tilly's tail snuck out and one by one it visited the Baker, the Woodcutter

and the Butcher,

and made sure they would NEVER tell the world about Tilly's terrible tale.

The FEMALE STORYTELLER grabs the book from the NARRATOR.

Throughout the following section the NARRATOR acts out the PLAYERS' dialogue with highly stylised physical actions.

MALE STORYTELLER: The next morning when Tilly awoke she found the terrified townspeople,

All talking about what had happened the night before.

FEMALE STORYTELLER: When Tilly heard she couldn't believe it was true,

And she ran all the way to the baker's shop to see it for herself.

MALE MUSICIAN: Tilly knew straight away that her tail was behind it all,

and in a fit of fear and fury she grabbed her tail and threw it into the baker's oven.

And with a great deep breath she slammed the big heavy door on to her tail,

hoping to break it off and free herself from its cruel clutches.

FEMALE STORYTELLER, MALE STORYTELLER & MALE MUSICIAN: SLAM, SLAM, SLAM!

FEMALE STORYTELLER: But the tail was too strong and the door didn't even make a dent.

So she ran to the woodcutter's cabin and grabbing his hatchet she started hacking away...

FEMALE STORYTELLER, MALE STORYTELLER & MALE MUSICIAN: HACK, HACK, HACK!

MALE MUSICIAN: But again her Tail was too tough and too tall
for her to chop,
and the axe blade just blunted and broke.

MALE STORYTELLER: So she sprinted to the butchers and
grabbed his big butcher's knife,
and tried to slice and sever her terrible tail...

FEMALE STORYTELLER, MALE STORYTELLER & MALE
MUSICIAN: SLICE, SLICE, SLICE

MALE STORYTELLER: but to no avail.

FEMALE STORYTELLER: It was as powerful as ever,
and she knew there was only one way to rid herself of her
terrible tail once and for all and that was to...

NARRATOR: (*Interrupting.*) – TELL THE TRUTH!
And so she told all the townspeople that she had an
important announcement to make.
And that she would meet them all at the town hall,
At noon on the dot!

Blackout – a bell rings – the PLAYERS speak in spotlight.

MALE MUSICIAN: Noon came.

FEMALE STORYTELLER: The clock struck.

MALE STORYTELLER: The bell rang and the crowd waited.

FEMALE MUSICIAN: They waited. And they waited. And they
waited.

*The bell finishes on its 12th ring, the lights fade back up but the
NARRATOR is nowhere to be seen.*

MALE STORYTELLER: But Tilly never came.

FEMALE STORYTELLER: And she was never seen again.

MALE MUSICIAN: So the townsfolk never really knew the total
truth.

FEMALE STORYTELLER: But many put two and two together.

MALE STORYTELLER: As for Tilly? Well some say the Tail took total control...

FEMALE STORYTELLER: ...And it now forces her to wander the world on a never-ending mission,

retelling all of her tallest tales to anyone who'll listen.

MALE STORYTELLER: Others say they went their separate ways,

and the tail now writes best-selling books and plays.

MALE MUSICIAN: Who knows?

FEMALE MUSICIAN: So if you're ever telling tales.

MALE MUSICIAN: And I hope you never do.

FEMALE STORYTELLER: Make sure those tales don't get too tall...

MALE STORYTELLER: ...and take control of *you*.

There is a banging noise from inside of the toy box from which the NARRATOR originally emerged.

Blackout.

END.

ERNEST AND THE PALE MOON

Gwendoline's area – Zoe Squire

Foreword

If *The Terrible Infants* is an homage to children's stories, then *Ernest and The Pale Moon* is my homage to horror stories. The wonderful, iconic works from masters such as Edgar Allan Poe to Alfred Hitchcock and also notably Steven Berkoff's adaptations of the former.

I wanted to take my experiences and what I'd learnt about storytelling on *The Terrible Infants* and apply that to a more adult subject matter. There is nothing more basic and primal than fear, harking back to the simplicity of telling ghost stories round the camp fire.

In the creation of *Ernest* I wanted to write a piece that allowed us to explore the many different types of fear and horror that are so prevalent within the genre; shock, suspense, violence, tension, gore and psychological horror to name but a few.

I also wanted a piece that allowed us to revel in the language and sound of the prose and explore classic horror aesthetics.

Like *The Terrible Infants*, when we entered the rehearsal room, *Ernest* was in prose form. So myself, director Emma Earle and the cast, set about distributing and shaping the story into an active theatrical form. One of the trickiest aspects was to keep the whole thing 'present' as the piece is written very much in the third person and often in past tense.

We analysed classic horror movies and texts – dissecting what we found scary, what made certain moments tense or terrifying, and we tried to find a way to fill our production with as many of these moments as we could.

At the same time we had to find a way to clearly deliver what is at times a very complicated narrative that is constantly jumping around in time and space.

Exhausting but exhilarating to perform, *Ernest* is a story of obsession, murder and a man's descent into madness; I hope you enjoy it.

Oliver Lansley

Director's Note

Ernest Hemel's descent into madness in *Ernest and the Pale Moon* is relentlessly tense; from the haunting cyclical counting of 'thirteen up, seven across,' to the visceral shock of the sound of bones cracking from within the walls. It's a ghoulish, macabre tale full of symbols, striking imagery and repetition, and one that proffers a multitude of staging possibilities.

Oliver and I met at National Youth Theatre and in 2008 I asked him to write me a 20-minute piece for a showcase of new writing and directing talent at Soho Theatre in London. We talked about wanting to do a gothic horror piece, somewhere between the films of Hitchcock and the short stories of Poe. He started by writing a short story in prose and I remember telling him it'd make a great film but would be a nightmare to stage. But undeterred, we spent a great deal of time bouncing the script back and forth; cutting or adding bits, re-ordering and re-imagining.

I enjoy making theatre with a heightened theatrical style and Oliver's script demands this. The resulting production was a fusion of text with innovative design, physical theatre, live music and stylised lighting. We worked with minimal props and set and constantly sought to make the narration active. This meant filling out spoken word moments with aural and visual elements, and in particular the live score provided by our actor musicians.

The rehearsal process was collaborative and experimental. We devoted a lot of time to exploring objects. On one occasion we spent over four hours working with two lengths of bamboo, determined to find a way of manipulating them to create the image of Gwendoline climbing the stairs. The aim was always to break through our first response to solving a moment and interrogate alternatives, for example a cello on its side with a blanket thrown over it being slowly lifted up and down to represent the rise and fall of a sleeping woman.

This approach led to an array of discoveries including creating a multi-faceted soundscape for Thomas' memory of war using Foley techniques, and realising that the set – an angular doorway in the mould of the German Expressionists set on a platform of perspective floorboards – would be even more exciting if it could rotate and then flip up on its end. Unlike a locked-off design process where the set design is fixed before rehearsals begin, our designer worked in parallel with us, able to respond fluidly to change and throw out or adapt existing ideas.

Ernest and the Pale Moon was a collaboration between my company Pins and Needles Productions and Les Enfants Terribles. In 2009 we took the show to Pleasance Above for the Edinburgh festival where we had a phenomenally successful run, selling out all shows, garnering a Total Theatre nomination and receiving a clutch of glowing reviews. An extensive UK tour followed in 2010 including venues such as Sheffield Theatres and Bristol Old Vic.

Emma Earle, Director

Gwendoline model – Zoe Squire

Costume sketches – Zoe Squire

Designer's Note

With any new design process comes the opportunity to open up a world of different ideas and new approaches to telling stories. When designing *Ernest* the question was how could I use these findings to capture each character's life, telling their physical and emotional journey and the various twists and turns, through a series of visual events and motifs.

The idea that all may not be what it at first seems was a concept I was interested in exploring further in my design process. I challenged myself to create a set that appeared to transform in front of the audiences' eyes, to unravel like the story. Forcing the audience to be privy to various events, becoming vouyeurs themselves as they watched Ernest from afar as he watched Gwendoline. In a similar vein to the script I was interested in the genre references and drawing upon these when looking at set and costume details; from Hitchcock's femme fatale to the German Expressionistic images from Edgar Allan Poe's short stories. How could we play with cinematic actions in a theatrical way on stage? Jumping between various locations, zooming in and out from snippets of each character's life running simultaneously to each other and regularly changing perspective. I worked with the idea of a constantly moving set that could be rotated, flipped and lit from within, instantly changing the settings and focus as quickly as the language did.

I love discovering unique ways to use props in my designs, to create exciting visuals that tell the story but also allow the audiences to reach into their own imagination and fill in the gaps. Illuminated lace umbrellas transformed into the moon, upturned cellos into sleeping bodies, sticks into walls, staircases and doors. Lighting and sound became as important in the final design concept as the images. Noir-inspired lighting mixed with an array of live Foley from a collection of both found objects and unique percussion instruments created an underscore and atmosphere to the action happening live on stage. Plastic bottles were twisted to create bone breaking sounds, trays of gravel suggested soldiers walking in the fields and torches became everything from stars and moons to reflections of flickering knives.

Ernest threw up lots of challenges to overcome and we went through various processes to get to its final design. How do you suggest an apartment is bleeding from its walls? How do you flip from scenes played in real time to stylistic vignettes like the Gwendoline and Thomas love story? How do you create a set that spirals with Ernest into madness?

But for all these questions we discovered many answers.

Zoe Squire, Designer

Storyboards – Zoe Squire

Costume sketches, 'Ernest' and 'Thomas' – Zoe Squire

ERNEST AND THE PALE MOON
2009 - 2010

THE TELEGRAPH ★ ★ ★ ★

A gloriously gothic production about obsession, from razor-sharp theatre group Les Enfants Terribles, this feels like Hitchcock's *Rear Window* meets Edgar Allan Poe, bubbling away in delight at the power of the imagination as the source of all our pleasures, but more importantly our woes... the real joy is the sheer inventiveness of the ensemble's quirky telling, combining physical and musical ingenuity to luminous effect.

THE STAGE – MUST SEE SHOW

There's a hypnotic quality to the production and a sense of deep traumas contained in some of its images. With some stunning *coups de theatre* and clever shifts in perspective, text and theatricality intersect in the work of a company very adept at showing how physicalised storytelling is at the heart of some of the best theatre around.

THE METRO ★ ★ ★ ★

As fresh as a new wound. The narrative jumps with lively, unusual imagery... This immersive, memorable piece spins with a sense of escalating evil... Right from the start, with sudden shouts and screams emanating from the darkness of an old gaol, it's clear that viewing the noirish new piece from theatre company Les Enfants Terrible is going to be a jumpy experience. A deliciously creepy thriller that draws heavily on Hitchcock's suspenseful *Rear Window* and Poe's macabre short stories...

YORK PRESS ★ ★ ★ ★ ★

It was all over in an hour of gothic storytelling as intense as absinthe... Since 2002, London company Les Enfants Terribles has been at the sharp end of such thrillingly piercing theatre, and Oliver Lansley's latest work is a deliciously dark delight... Atmosphere is all in *Ernest and the Pale Moon*... it made for the most visually memorable night's theatre your reviewer has experienced this year with an increasing, if strangely pleasurable, discomfort.

THE LIST ★ ★ ★ ★

Writer Oliver Lansley has once again reached into his wonderfully twisted mind for this dark gem... As the characters' lives intersect, the framework of a gothic horror story provides escalating tension, as well as the requisite twists and turns, until the stage is awash with (imaginary) blood and audiences' hearts are in their mouths. It takes a skilled company to transport an audience into such an unsettling and complete world and then bundle them back safely into the 'real' one... a complex, self-contained experience that, once over, feels like a half-remembered, lingering dream.

FRINGE REVIEW ★ ★ ★ ★ ★

Visually this show is stunning. Reminiscent of a Francis Bacon painting, the set is so imaginatively deployed that it does as much to further the tale unfolding as do the characters... This show is endlessly inventive in the methods it uses in its storytelling... there is no movement or sound that does not further the dramatic tension or add another layer to the story unfolding... This really is a tremendous show from a very confident and inventive young company, really setting the standard for what can be achieved within the restrictions of the Fringe. Tightly scripted, beautifully staged and inventively realised, this is a definite five-star show.

TOTAL THEATRE – AWARD NOMINEE

From the opening image of a white-faced man leaping to his feet in panic, *Ernest and the Pale Moon* hooks us with a well-paced and beautifully staged creepy faux-historical tale of Ernest – a man locked up in a dark insane asylum for a murder of horrific proportions. Drawing on the worlds of Tim Burton, Edgar Allen Poe and classic mime, the play is an atmospheric and riveting physical theatre experience.

'Ernest' and 'Gwendoline' model – Zoe Squire

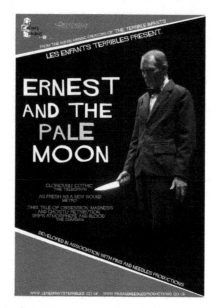

Ernest and the Pale Moon was originated as a twenty-minute piece at Soho Theatre for Director Emma Earle's 'Director's Cuts' showcase. It was then further developed into a full-length piece and premiered in Pleasance Above at the 2009 Edinburgh Fringe Festival. The production was a collaboration between Les Enfants Terribles Theatre Company and Pins and Needles Productions.

The Cast were:
ERNEST HEMEL / CHORUS 1 – Oliver Lansley
GWENDOLINE BERTRAM / CHORUS 2 – Grace Carter
EDGEFORD / THOMAS THISTLE / OFFICER /
CHORUS 3 – Joe Woolmer
NURSE / MOTHER / CHORUS 4 – Rachel Dawson

For the subsequent tour the part of GWENDOLINE was played by Nicole Lewis and the part of THOMAS THISTLE was played by Dan Wheeler.

Director – Emma Earle
Designer – Zoe Squire
Lighting Designer – Paul Green
Music – Tomas Gisby
Additional music and orchestration – Rachel Dawson

Note. Some chorus lines may be redistributed throughout the chorus to suit staging requirements.

1. ERNEST WATCHING

ERNEST sits in his chair at his window as the audience enter. His face is barely lit. The sound of a clock ticking and the occasional creak of ERNEST's apartment. A sudden flash of light. ERNEST is pressed up against the window with a wild look on his face. Blackout.

Pre-recorded musical introduction into '**ASYLUM AMBIENCE**'

2. ASYLUM 1

Ambient sound of Asylum.

Langshotts Asylum. NURSE and EDGEFORD – they pass by various cells. NURSE carries a lamp.

NURSE: First time in a place like this?

EDGEFORD: Sorry? Oh, yes, no, I mean… In a place like *this* yes, but obviously I've been to countless other institutions before.

He looks around uneasily.

EDGEFORD: Can they hear us?

NURSE: They could if they chose, most don't.

NURSE mimes opening cell 1, EDGEFORD peers inside. We hear the sound of a muttering inmate.

They continue to walk for a while, passing cells.

NURSE: May I ask how you do it?

EDGEFORD: Do what?

NURSE: Make your judgements… How you decide whether a man is truly mad or not.

EDGEFORD: Well it's a complicated process.

NURSE: Doesn't seem complicated to me. This lot, all of 'em, mad as the day is long. Dangerous. Not sure why an 'assessment' is necessary, when they're dribbling like babies and howling like wolves.

EDGEFORD: Well the mind is a complicated beast Miss...

NURSE: ...Green.

EDGEFORD: Miss Green. They may seem damaged or disturbed but that does not mean to say they cannot be fixed.

NURSE opens another cell. A scream followed by an inmate spitting at EDGEFORD.

NURSE: There's no fixing to be done here I can assure you. You clean 'em up and put 'em back out there, they'll just find a way back in, you mark my words.

They reach ERNEST's cell and look in.

NURSE: Here he is. Ernest Hemel.

'SINGING BOWL'.

EDGEFORD stares at him. NURSE is visibly unsettled.

EDGEFORD: What's he done with the window?

NURSE: We had to cover it up. At night he would just scream and scream and start tearing at the walls, scratching, scraping. He would damage himself quite badly, we'd have to sedate him and strap him up, took us a while to figure out it was the light of the moon he was afraid of. We covered the window and he's not made a peep since.

EDGEFORD stares at the man.

NURSE: That's how he was found, like that... pale as a ghost... like he's been scared to death. Timid fella to look at him now but when you hear about what he done... Well like they say... the quiet ones...

Lights change. Pre-recorded musical introduction.

Once actors are in position, metronome starts.

ERNEST: Tick tock tick tock tick tock… Ticked the clock as Ernest Hemel sat, quiet and still in the darkened corner of his apartment block.

'LIVE MUSIC BEGINS – ERNEST'S THEME'

CHORUS 3: No light but a slight dusting from the distant moon. Still, still he sat,

ERNEST: calm and patient

CHORUS 3: as he watched, rapt, from his window.

CHORUS 4: Eyes straining as they peered across the empty void to reach their goal.

CHORUS 3: No movement but the occasional twitch from his clammy hand, restless, revealing the inner itch that lay beneath the calm waters in which his body bathed.

CHORUS 4: Tick tock,

CHORUS 3: tick tock,

ERNEST: tick tock, ticked past nine on the clock

CHORUS 4: counting down the precious remaining minutes of this wonderful vision.

ERNEST: Love.

CHORUS 4: He called it to himself.

ERNEST: Devotion. A quiet, admirable devotion, which would one day be embraced.

CHORUS 3: For his eyes were felt, he knew that much. He was but one party in this game which was shared with another.

ERNEST: She felt him, he knew it.

CHORUS 3: And every night she would sit for him, as he watched her, in the darkness.

ERNEST: So still, almost like a painting, her clean white skin, the long flow of her hair glowing under the light of the pale moon.

CHORUS 3: They both played their parts, most willingly.

CHORUS 4: Waiting, each alone but not alone as the ticking clock counted down the moments of their nightly encounter.

CHORUS 3: He would sometimes forget to breathe.

Metronome stops.

CHORUS 3: His eyes travelling across the emptiness to embrace her fully. He held her tightly and dreamt of her touch.

ERNEST: She belonged to him.

Lights change.

4. ASYLUM 2

NURSE's lamp on.

'ASYLUM AMBIENCE'

EDGEFORD: Does he ever speak?

NURSE: Not to me, he just sits there, staring at that picture of his.

EDGEFORD: Who's the woman in the picture?

NURSE: I believe it's his mother… Some have said that it's the young girl they found but that's probably just stories. You get a lot of that in this place, people talking, it's as if the truth isn't enough for some people.

Lights change.

5. GWENDOLINE INTRODUCTION

GWENDOLINE BERTRAM sits in her den. We can see her through a lace shroud, lit by candlelight.

'GWENDOLINE'S THEME' *sung – continued by accordion.*

CHORUS 1: Miss Gwendoline Bertram.

CHORUS 4: A most divine creature…

CHORUS 1: A most exquisite young maiden…

CHORUS 4: …glanced around at the hundreds of burnt out candles that covered her room, each one a different beautiful wax figurine that had become crooked and disfigured as the candle had melted. She looked down at the figure in her hand –

GWENDOLINE: – sparkling away like her very own special star.

CHORUS 1: The stars were shy in the city in which she lived. Veiled by gas and steam and smoke and cloud. Reticent to be seen clearly for fear they may be snared and snatched from their hiding places.

GWENDOLINE: But not the bright moon.

CHORUS 1: Gwendoline sat quietly, as she did every night, waiting for the moon to pierce the horizon of the foreboding apartment block that sat across from her window, still and menacing like a heavy hound abandoned by its master.

CHORUS 4: She felt a finger of moonlight reach down and caress her face. She smiled, blew out the candle and pulled open the curtains of her apartment window to let the light embrace her.

GWENDOLINE appears from behind the lace. She looks up at the moon which is represented by a torch shone through a lace parasol.

GWENDOLINE: She loved the moon.

CHORUS 4: Its glow was like a balm to her broken eyes, not like the harsh, cruel sun. Her captor that kept her locked up inside.

Too cruel for her porcelain skin, too strong for her gentle, misted eyes.

Clouded pearls that felt shape and form and light but could barely see past the confines of her room.

6. ERNEST WATCHES GWENDOLINE

'ERNEST'S THEME'

ERNEST: Unlike the sharp, hawk-like eyes that were trained upon her as she sat, smiling gently.

CHORUS 3: She was unaware of his invasive gaze that clutched her tightly in her seat.

CHORUS 4: She couldn't see into the dark window of the dark building that loomed beyond her sight.

CHORUS 3: She couldn't see that in that darkness sat a man.

ERNEST: Still, calm, patient. Watching.

CHORUS 4: Looking at her with as much love as she looked upon her moon.

ERNEST: He watched her,

GWENDOLINE: as she watched her moon,

CHORUS 4: and the clock ticked and tocked.

ERNEST: Tick tock, tick tock,

CHORUS 4: until the time was up.

Blackout.

7. THOMAS INTRODUCTION

'THOMAS THISTLE'S THEME' – *on harmonica and then on cello.*

CHORUS 1: Next door sat a young man,

CHORUS 2: Thomas Thistle,

CHORUS 1: Cursing the shrapnel that peppered the flesh of his thigh and the pain that clutched at his leg with the stubby fingers of a scared child.

CHORUS 2: He had spent much of his time alone in the month since his discharge from the army.

CHORUS 1: Struggling at first to cope with the sprawling randomness of life outside the military.
Faced with a terrifying, oppressive freedom and the heaving lack of purpose that hung like an albatross around the neck of one's everyday existence.

CHORUS 2: He longed for some form of companionship, a distraction, and seeing the face of the young lady who lived next door had lifted his heart higher than it had been since moving into the building.

THOMAS: He had never seen anything like her.

CHORUS 2: Her shock of soft white hair cascading like snowdrops from her shoulders. Her skin, so white, almost translucent, but sublime in its purity, like a china doll.

THOMAS: And those eyes…

CHORUS 1: He held the small wax figure he had spent so much time carving tightly in his hand and stared at it.

THOMAS: She is so close.

CHORUS 2: His eyes bored into the walls as if through sheer will they would be able to pierce them and rest upon her face.

THOMAS: He dreamt of her…

'He placed his hand against the window' – Karen Scott

GWENDOLINE: As she watched her moon…

ERNEST: And as she was watched from the dark window of the dark building…

CHORUS 4: After a moment, he grabbed his stick and rose to his feet.

THOMAS crosses to GWENDOLINE's area.

THOMAS: Knock knock knock.

8. GWENDOLINE HEARS A KNOCK AT THE DOOR

GWENDOLINE: Tick tock,

CHORUS 4: tick tock,

CHORUS 1: tick tock,

GWENDOLINE: ticked the clock as Gwendoline Bertram sat, quiet and still watching her moon.

THOMAS: Knock knock knock

GWENDOLINE: Gwendoline's heart leapt when she heard the knocking at her door.
She wasn't used to visitors.

CHORUS 4: She called out…

GWENDOLINE: Hello?

CHORUS 4: …and was greeted by a warm, rich voice.

THOMAS: Hello.

GWENDOLINE: Wings of butterflies beat in her stomach.

CHORUS 1: Her hand trembled slightly with excitement.
She rose to her feet and opened the door.

CHORUS 4: And there she found him.
The man whom for some reason she had not been able to shake from her thoughts.

CHORUS 1: She smiled.

GWENDOLINE: Hello.

THOMAS: Oh, hello, er my name is Thomas Thistle, I'm from next door.

GWENDOLINE: Oh, yes. I remember… My name is Gwendoline.

THOMAS: I was, well it's silly really I just… Well I wondered if you might want some company?

Lights change.

9. ERNEST WATCHES GWENDOLINE LEAVE HER WINDOW SEAT

Metronome starts.

ERNEST: Tick tock,

CHORUS 4: tick tock,

CHORUS 3: tick tock,

CHORUS 2: tick tock,

ERNEST: ticked the clock as Ernest Hemel sat, quiet and still watching Miss Gwendoline Bertram watch the moon.

ALL CHORUS: Knock knock knock

CHORUS 4: The index finger of his right hand twitched as her eyes dropped their gaze for a moment.

CHORUS 2: She turned her head a fraction, to listen.

ERNEST: She spoke.

CHORUS 3: Ernest could not hear the words nor guess what they were.
He couldn't even imagine the sounds of them in her mouth as she spoke, having never heard her voice. This fact ached inside him.

CHORUS 4: His hand clenched as she rose to her feet.

He shifted very slightly, as she moved towards the door.

ERNEST: He looked at his clock

ALL CHORUS: tick tock, tick tock

CHORUS 3: He rose from his chair and placed his hand against the window, his heart racing like a mother who had lost her child on a crowded street.

CHORUS 2: His clammy fingers left fingerprints upon the glass as he stared and stared.

ERNEST: Movement.

A man.

The CHORUS play the following exchange into ERNEST's ear, as if it is being played out in his own head, thus the intonation is changed from before.

GWENDOLINE: Hello.

THOMAS: Oh, hello, er my name is Thomas Thistle, I'm from next door.

GWENDOLINE: Oh, yes. I remember… My name is Gwendoline.

THOMAS: I was, well it's silly really I just… Well I wondered if you might want some company?

ERNEST: Ernest forgot to breathe, his heart thundered in his chest. Pounding as if trying to escape. Her eyes on him. Her moon was forgotten. She smiled.

Metronome stops.

ERNEST: Ernest had never seen that smile.

'ERNEST'S THEME'

CHORUS 3: Blood seared through his veins as a familiar rage began to engulf his being.

CHORUS 2: He pressed his face up against the window.

CHORUS 4: His now, boiling breath, heaving and wheezing and clouding the glass.

CHORUS 2: His hands now clenched to fists, shaking slightly.

ERNEST: He watched as they spoke words he could not hear, as they exchanged looks, laughs, he would never understand.

CHORUS 4: Ernest's eyes welled with tears of fury and he hammered his fist on his window, once.
As he did so his mind flicked to the body of his mother, sleeping gently nearby.

ERNEST: He didn't want to wake her.

CHORUS 4: He strained his ears, heard no sounds of stirring and so returned to his watch.
His breath unsteady like an animal.

THOMAS: The man left.

GWENDOLINE: Gwendoline returned to her darkness.

CHORUS 4: And the moon rose in the sky.

Lights change.

'BLOOD THEME INTO THOMAS' THEME'

10. THOMAS RETURNS TO HIS APARTMENT

THOMAS: Thomas Thistle bade Miss Gwendoline Bertram goodnight. He was almost unaware of the pain in his leg that followed him around like a starving dog. It had been silenced by his happiness, pacified by contentment. He moved to his window and switched on his light.

11. ERNEST WITH KNIFE IN WINDOW

ERNEST: A light appeared in another window.

CHORUS 4: Ernest saw the face of a man.

ERNEST: The man he had been cursing, the man he didn't know.

CHORUS 2: A tiny droplet of blood slid down the crease between Ernest's left thumb and forefinger as he slowly unclenched his fist, allowing his nails to slide out from the grooves they had created in his palm.

CHORUS 4: In his right hand he could feel the weight of the knife he had snatched from his kitchen drawer moments before.

CHORUS 2: His breath deepened.

THOMAS: The man smiled and sighed.

ERNEST: Ernest flinched as the man seemed to stare directly at him, but he knew he could not be seen. Could he?

Lights change.

12. LIGHT SHINES IN THOMAS' FACE

THOMAS: Thomas stared out of the window, a contented smile upon his face, until something caught his eye.

Torch light on THOMAS' face – CHORUS 2.

CHORUS 2: He blinked, momentarily blinded.
From a dark window of the dark building that overshadowed his apartment a light was flickering upon his face.

CHORUS 4: He strained his eyes trying to detect the source of this light but whenever he thought he might be able to make out the shape of a figure, it struck him again, blinding him momentarily and flushing his eyes out of focus.
Flickering purposefully upon his face. Fluttering intently around his eyes like a moth around a flame.

THOMAS: A signal? A warning? A cry for help?

CHORUS 4: Thomas rested on his stick and counted the blocks of the building.

The pulse of the cello counts along with him.

THOMAS: One, two, three, four, five, six, seven, eight, nine, ten, eleven, twelve,
thirteen floors up.

One, two, three, four, five, six, seven across. On the corner.

13. ERNEST SEES A DARK FIGURE CROSS BELOW

CHORUS 2: Ernest's heart was racing as the man in the building opposite stared directly at him.

ERNEST: How could he see him? How could he know?

CHORUS 4: The knife in his right hand trembled as the moon high above shone down upon him and its light caught the blade.

CHORUS 2 – torch on THOMAS' face.
ERNEST holds torch to represent light flickering from knife.

THOMAS: Thomas stood for another second, staring at the source of the light, he then turned and walked out of his room.

ERNEST: He is coming.

CHORUS 2 – torch off.

CHORUS 4: Ernest stood in the dark and waited.
His breath heavy as his nostrils filled with the pungent scent of the fresh hot-house flowers that sat, as they always did, in the vase on the table beneath his mother's portrait.

ERNEST: He waited. Tick tock tick tock.

CHORUS 3: Ernest's heart began to pound. He pushed himself up against his window to get a view of the ground between the two apartment blocks and he waited.

CHORUS 2: Thirteen floors below he saw a dark figure move towards his building.

He clutched his knife tightly in his hand and moved to his door.

ERNEST: He is coming.

ERNEST – torch off.
Cast move structure – the window has now become the door.

CHORUS 3: There was a knock.

CHORUS 2: (*Using a stick to create a knocking sound.*) Knock, knock, knock.

ERNEST: Ernest stared at his door as the knocks echoed through his bones.

CHORUS 2: (*Using a stick to create a knocking sound.*) Knock, knock, knock.

ERNEST: He is here.

CHORUS 2: Ernest moved to the door and reached for the handle.

CHORUS 3: Ernest pushed himself up against the wall and opened the door.

LX under floorboards on.

CHORUS 3: He listened and tried to remain still, he could hear the heavy breath of the figure on the other side.

ERNEST: One step, two steps.

CHORUS 3: Footsteps crossed the threshold.

ERNEST: Three steps, four steps, five steps.

CHORUS 2: Ernest's heart thundered in his chest, his knuckles whitened around the knife in his hand. Beetles of sweat scuttled across his brow.

ERNEST: Six steps, seven…

CHORUS 2: Ernest slammed the door shut and launched himself upon the figure, plunging his knife deep into the back, feeling its blade scrape slightly against fragments of spine.

CHORUS 3: A small searching glow of moonlight crept into Ernest's apartment.

ERNEST: His heart stopped when he caught sight of the shock of white hair that fell into his arms.

'BLOOD THEME' – *action rewinds.*

Lights change.

14. GWENDOLINE FOLLOWS HER STAR

CHORUS 1: As Gwendoline went to close her curtains something caught her eye.

CHORUS 1 flickers torch light on her face.

GWENDOLINE: A flash, a sparkle, like a star twinkling just for her.

CHORUS 1: She gazed out, her failing eyes struggling to find their target. The star remained, twinkling brightly, shining into her eyes.

GWENDOLINE: Her very own special star.

CHORUS 3: Its light caressed her face. It was calling to her.

GWENDOLINE: Another gift?

CHORUS 3: She smiled.

CHORUS 1: It came from a dark window of the dark building across from hers.
Straining her eyes to make out the shapes of the windows she counted the blocks of the building.

Counting on cello.

GWENDOLINE: One, two, three, four, five, six, seven, eight, nine, ten, eleven, twelve,

thirteen floors up.

One, two, three, four, five, six, seven across. On the corner.

CHORUS 1: She remained there in the darkness for a moment longer watching the twinkling star, before turning and walking out of her apartment.

CHORUS 1 torch off. CHORUS 3 torch on – the two of them play a game with GWENDOLINE, teasing her with the light.

CHORUS 3: Clutching the railings, she made her way down the stairs and out into the night.

Night SFX.

CHORUS 1: As she crossed the space between the two buildings she looked up and saw the moon high up in the sky, shining down upon her.

CHORUS 3: She followed the star…

CHORUS 1: all the way…

CHORUS 3: …to the entrance of the building. She started climbing the stairs.

Sticks are used by CHORUS 3 and CHORUS 1 to represent the stairs and doors.

GWENDOLINE: One, two, three, four, five, six, seven, eight, nine, ten, eleven, twelve,

thirteen floors up.

CHORUS 3: She counted the doors.

GWENDOLINE: One, two, three, four, five, six...six...six...six... Seven across. On the corner.

CHORUS 3: She knocked.

CHORUS 3: Knock, knock, knock.

GWENDOLINE: Nothing.

CHORUS 3: Knock, knock, knock.

GWENDOLINE: Nothing.

CHORUS 3: Knock, knock, knock.

GWENDOLINE: Nothing.

CHORUS 4: She turned to leave but as she did she heard the gentle creak of a door opening.

LX under floorboards on.

CHORUS 4: She stared inside the dark apartment. She could see nothing but the thick darkness. She stepped forward.

ERNEST: One step, two steps.

GWENDOLINE: Crossing the threshold.

ERNEST: Three steps, four steps, five steps.

GWENDOLINE: She looked around, trying to find her star.

ERNEST: Six steps, seven…

CHORUS 3: Gwendoline's eyes opened wide as she felt the knife enter her back, her mouth dropped open as she struggled to breathe.

CHORUS 4: She could not scream, her lungs refusing to inflate as they snatched at the stale air of the apartment.

'BLOOD THEME' – *action rewinds.*
Lights change.

15. THOMAS WITNESSES THE STABBING

Fast music played on the cello creating sense of urgency.

CHORUS 1: Thomas Thistle exited his room and moved to the dresser in his hallway. Kneeling down he rifled through the drawers and began pulling out the junk inside.

CHORUS 2: There was an urgency to his actions, a strange feeling in the pit of his stomach fueling his curiosity.

THOMAS: Anxiety pricked at the hairs on his neck and back.

CHORUS 1: From behind walls of bric-à-brac he uncovered a small tin box.

THOMAS: He opened the box, a tobacco tin, some letters, photographs…

CHORUS 1: His military issue handgun.

CHORUS 2: Thomas froze like a child confronted with the ghost of a long forgotten fear.

THOMAS: The gun which had never been fired.

Sudden stab on cello.

CHORUS 1: He suddenly felt a sharp pain in his right leg, a scream from the shard of shrapnel that was now becoming a piece of him.

CHORUS 2: Biting away his pain he pushed the handgun aside and retrieved the old pair of binoculars that he sought.

THOMAS: He pulled out his handkerchief and wiped the years of dust from their lenses before heaving himself to his feet and returning to his room.

CHORUS 2: He walked to his window and counted the blocks of the building.

THOMAS: One, two, three, four, five, six, seven, eight, nine, ten, eleven, twelve,
thirteen floors up.

One, two, three, four, five, six, seven across. On the corner.

CHORUS 4: His hands clutched the handle of his cane tightly as he raised the binoculars to his eyes and looked into the dark window of the dark building.
A small shaft of moonlight crept inside the apartment.

THOMAS: He saw her, pale as a ghost, her long white hair resting gently on her shoulders.

ERNEST: One step, two steps.

THOMAS: She crossed the threshold.

ERNEST: Three steps, four steps, five steps.

THOMAS: She looked around.

CHORUS 4: Thomas thought he could make out the shadow of a figure behind her.

ERNEST: Six steps, seven…

CHORUS 4: The flash of the blade caught the moonlight blinding him.

Flash of light and blackout – the CHORUS breathe heavily, mirroring THOMAS' panic.

THOMAS: He dropped the binoculars, his heart raced.
What had he witnessed? It couldn't be…?
With shaking hands he scrambled around on the floor to pick up his father's binoculars.
thirteen floors up.
Seven across. On the corner.
He returned the binoculars to his fearful eyes.

Lights up.

'ERNEST'S THEME'

CHORUS 4: Thomas saw the face of a man, staring back at him. Eyes cold as stone, full of hate.

ERNEST: With hot blood on his hands, Ernest saw the man, the man whom should now be dying in his arms, standing there, in the opposing apartment watching him.
He drew his curtains shut.

Lights change.

Pre-recorded music – ERNEST's record. ERNEST's apartment is created – portrait frame is hung, flowers and table placed.

Throughout the scene CHORUS 2 and CHORUS 4 provide sound effects in a Foley style.

CHORUS 4: (*Knocking SFX.*) knock, knock, knock

ERNEST: Hello?

OFFICER: Mr Hemel?

ERNEST: Yes?

OFFICER: I'm sorry to bother you at this time but we've had a report of a disturbance coming from your apartment.

ERNEST: A disturbance?

OFFICER: That's right. I wonder if I could ask you a few questions.

ERNEST: Questions? What sort of questions?

OFFICER: May I come in?

ERNEST: Yes, of course.

ERNEST opens the door and lets the OFFICER in.

OFFICER: Nice place.

ERNEST: Thank you.

OFFICER: Yours?

ERNEST: Yes. Can I get you anything? A drink?

OFFICER: A drink, maybe a hot drink thank you, if it's not too much trouble.

ERNEST: Tea perhaps?

OFFICER: Yes, tea would be most sufficient.

ERNEST leaves the room to make the tea, leaving the OFFICER to look around. ERNEST constantly tries to keep his eye on the OFFICER as he makes the tea.

ERNEST: It may take a few moments for the kettle to boil. The water here is always very cold.

OFFICER: Quite.

ERNEST crosses to the kitchen.

ERNEST: May I ask what questions…

OFFICER: We have had reports of a disturbance.

ERNEST: What sort of disturbance?

OFFICER: Are these curtains always closed?

ERNEST: Often. When it's dark out.

OFFICER: Are you alone?

ERNEST: How do you mean?

OFFICER: Have you had company this evening?

ERNEST: No I…

OFFICER: Reports of a pale young lady.

ERNEST: A pale lady?

ERNEST reaches into his kitchen drawer and pulls out a knife.

ERNEST: What's happened to her?

Beat.

OFFICER: What's that smell?

ERNEST: The flowers.

The OFFICER stares at the flowers, then up at a spot on the wall.

OFFICER: A fine looking woman.

ERNEST: Excuse me?

'The Officer Scene' – Karen Scott

OFFICER: The painting… (*To himself.*) A pale lady… Your wife?

ERNEST: My mother… She's asleep in the next room.

OFFICER: I thought you said you were alone.

ERNEST: I am alone, she sleeps through. She's not well. I could show you if you like.

ERNEST shows the OFFICER to his mother's room – see the cello lying on its side, covered by a sheet, to represent sleeping mother.

ERNEST: I'd rather not wake her if that's ok with you, she's not well.

OFFICER: Of course.

As the OFFICER looks into the room ERNEST produces the knife from behind his back and moves towards the OFFICER. We hear the old-fashioned whistling of a kettle boiling. ERNEST hides the knife behind his back as the OFFICER turns.

ERNEST: That's the kettle. I should get you your tea.

Lights change.

17. ASYLUM 3

'ASYLUM AMBIENCE'

THOMAS: So it was Thomas who called the police?

NURSE: I believe so, yes. Said he'd witnessed a murder. That he'd seen a young girl killed. But this was several days before Ernest was brought in.

THOMAS: So what happened?

NURSE: The officer reported that he thought him to be a quiet, polite man, sane as a judge – normal, calm, helpful. He said the man he brought in several days later could have been a different person all together. He described him as a shell, a cadaver of the man he met that night.

EDGEFORD: Really? And there was no sign of the girl?

NURSE: None, not at that time, he said he found Mr Hemel to be most helpful.

EDGEFORD: So what happened in those few days that passed?

NURSE: Who knows?

EDGEFORD: It just doesn't make any sense. How could a normal, seemingly sane human being have been turned into... this... in a matter of mere days?

NURSE: Guilt? It'll always catch up with you in the end. A relentless pursuer, you can ignore, bury it, run from it, but it'll just keep hunting you down, it'll never stop till it's dragged you into its blackness.

Lights change.

18. ERNEST PUTS MOTHER IN THE WALL

In the scene change, the portrait returns to above mother's bed. Sound effects are provided by the CHORUS to accompany the action of the scene.

CHORUS 2: Tap tap, tap tap, tap tap. (*SFX.*)
With the warm blood of his victim still on his hands
Tap tap (*SFX.*)
Ernest reached up to the wall and slowly and delicately
Tap tap (*SFX.*)
He searched for the right spot.
Tap tap, tap tap, tap tap... (*SFX – on the third set of taps the SFX changes to sound hollow.*)

CHORUS 3: When he heard the sound of a hollow his hand stopped.

CHORUS 2: Calmly and with utmost precision, Ernest began to peel back the wallpaper.

CHORUS 3: He carefully removed the nails from the boards beneath, one by one,
then began prising away the planks to reveal the musty dark void that lay between the walls.

He looked inside.

ERNEST: Black, empty, dead.

CHORUS 2: Ernest looked upon his victim. The shocking red blood screaming against the soft whiteness of her hair and skin.

CHORUS 3: Ernest's heart was thundering, his mind was racing. A momentary flood of emotion tried to engulf him but he held it back.

CHORUS 2: He took hold of her.

CHORUS 3: She was light and limp in his hands as he placed her into the cavity.

Places CHORUS 4 in cavity. ERNEST crushes her body into place – Bone crunching SFX (made by plastic bottle).

CHORUS 2: He forced her body into the darkness, crushing her elegant limbs into their claustrophobic resting place. She didn't put up a fight as her body was bent and broken and forced into place.

CHORUS 3: He looked at her pale face one last time, sweat christening his brow, hands shaking with fear and rage and shame.
He kissed her cool lips.

CHORUS 2: At his touch she stirred, as if waking from a deep sleep, her eyes opened and she looked at him, fear swimming in her eyes. She tried to scream but she couldn't, her body wouldn't allow it. Her hand reached out and grabbed him, a desperate plea, a last call for clemency.

CHORUS 3: Ernest's heart ripped through his chest, his eyes wide, he tore her tight fingers from his shirt.

CHORUS 2: He looked into her eyes and she looked into his, both now fully grasping the horror of the situation.

With one final horrifying crunch ERNEST forces her into the cavity and moves away.

CHORUS 3: He heard a terrible sound coming from her throat, a sound unlike any he had ever heard before. Animalistic, primal, a dying spirit inside a broken body.

Beat – CHORUS 4 starts to make a gasping sound, which builds slowly until it becomes a horrifying scream.

CHORUS: He then began replacing the planks.

CHORUS 2: He hammered in the nails.

LX slow fade to black. Tilt structure (floorboards up). The CHORUS create sound effects for the following, through the blackness.

CHORUS 3: He heard her nails scratching against the wood…
Like trapped rats.
The harsh, blunt cracks as her soft nails snapped and splintered against the wood.
The dull sound of the numb stumps of her fingers, prising at the boards.

The SFX build to a crescendo then stop.

ERNEST: It stopped.

Lights under floorboards on.

CHORUS 4: Slowly, as if approaching a dangerous creature, he edged closer to the wall, pressing his face up against it to listen.
Through the wood he could just make out the sound of death. The last drops of steam rising from a kettle's mouth.

CHORUS 2: A gentle gasp, a dying breath, death's rattle.

ERNEST: It had ended.

Lights change.

'FAST MUSIC'

CHORUS 4: He wiped the knife and returned it to his drawer.

CHORUS 2: He mopped up the blood from his wooden floors.

CHORUS 4: He changed his bloody clothes.

CHORUS 2: And washed his hands.

CHORUS 4: Ernest stared at the blank wall. A long shaft of moonlight, the shape of a casket, crept through his curtains, outlining the place where her body lay.

CHORUS 2: Slowly he began to notice a tiny speck appearing in the middle of it.

ERNEST: Miniscule, a pin prick, a small insect.

ERNEST moves towards the upright structure, now representing a wall.

CHORUS 4: Ernest stared at the spot, fear swelling in his stomach.

Fearfully he reached out a finger and touched it

ERNEST: It was wet and hot.

ERNEST turns to reveal blood on his hands.

'FAST MUSIC'

CHORUS 2: Overcome with fear Ernest ran to his mother's bedroom.

He grabbed the portrait that hung above her bed and, with urgency and panic he covered the damned spot that had appeared to torment him.

ERNEST hangs the portrait on the structure.

CHORUS 4: He stepped back.

ERNEST: He clenched his fist to prevent his hands from shaking.

CHORUS 2: They retained a slight redness, a flush that would never leave them.

CHORUS 4: Ernest stared into the eyes of his mother...

The clock ticked...

Clock chime SFX.

Lights change.

'Through the wood he could just make out the sound of death'
– Karen Scott

THOMAS and GWENDOLENE's themes played on glockenspiels.

The following story is enacted as a dumbshow with music and narration. THOMAS and GWENDOLENE appear from behind the structure, performing their actions like a mechanical cuckoo clock.

CHORUS 1: It was a crisp Autumn evening when Thomas Thistle first laid eyes upon Gwendoline Bertram.

Before then he had no idea who inhabited the apartment next door.

The only sign of life was the occasional sound through the thin walls and the large white candles that would appear on the doormat, at the beginning of each week, like clockwork, before disappearing never to be seen again.

CHORUS 4: Gwendoline lived by candlelight. Her eyes were too sensitive for the harsh glare of day and so she would spend her existence locked up inside her small apartment, with only a single lit candle for her to see her way.

This candle would be delivered to her door each week, like clockwork.

CHORUS 1: The candles fascinated Thomas and on this particular Autumn evening he had been overcome with curiosity and had stationed himself at his door waiting, staring through the tiny peephole at the large white candle sitting expectantly on the opposing doormat.

He waited there patiently...

CHORUS 4: Gwendoline shuffled through the darkness of her apartment as she did, every week, to fetch her candle. She opened her door and the aggressive light of the hallway attacked her sense. She groped around on the doormat for her candle

CHORUS 1: Thomas saw her, for the first time.

He had never seen anything like her.

Those eyes.

Clock chimes – they retreat.

CHORUS 1: The very next day Thomas ventured out and purchased a large white candle.

He spent days carefully carving it, ever so delicately with the razor sharp edge of his military issue pocket knife into the image of the pale young lady.

When the day came he went to his door and opened it, and peering around cautiously, he reached down and replaced the large white candle with his own before returning to his peephole to wait.

CHORUS 4: As always Gwendoline went to her door to fetch her candle, she opened the door and clutched around in the brightness. As her fingers touched it she stopped for a moment. She gently glided her hands over the moulded wax, feeling the contours Thomas had painstakingly carved.

CHORUS 1: Thomas watched on eagerly, almost forgetting to breathe. He saw what seemed to be the soft shadow of a smile appear across her lips.

Hurriedly he pulled open the door.

CHORUS 4: Through the piercing light, she saw him.

CHORUS 1: They stared into each other's eyes.

CHORUS 4: Their hearts stopped.

CHORUS 1: Clocks didn't tick.

CHORUS 4: Suddenly Gwendoline regained herself…

Clock chimes.

CHORUS 4: …and shuffled back into her apartment.

They retreat.

CHORUS 1: This same ritual continued for months, every week another perfectly carved visage of her beauty.

CHORUS 4: …and every week she would remain at the door a tiny moment longer as if she were aware of his gaze and was rewarding him for his kindness.

CHORUS 1: They would long to speak,

CHORUS 4: to say hello

CHORUS 1: but each time they would remain there still, silent,

CHORUS 4: watching through their peepholes.

CHORUS 1: Until one day Thomas decided to knock on her door.

THOMAS: Knock knock knock.

Lights change. Move structure.

20. SLEEP DEPRIVATION

THOMAS: Thomas Thistle sat, minutes, hours, days, nights, in the darkness, watching the apartment thirteen up, seven across. Hoping to catch a glimpse of his love. He begged to go back, to change things. Another loss, another death, caused by his inaction. He saw nothing but her absence.

ERNEST: Ernest Hemel sat, minutes, hours, days, nights, staring at the picture of his mother that hung upon his wall, a cenotaph heralding an unmarked tomb. A shadow of crimson seemed to creep out from behind every side of its thick frame. The sounds of scratching pricked in his ears. He forgot to breathe, or move, or eat, he just sat there, staring at the portrait, fingernails digging deep into the arms of his chair.

THOMAS: The days passed and Thomas stared at Ernest

ERNEST: And Ernest stared at the picture
And the picture stared back.

LX flash of light on shining mother in picture frame.

ERNEST: His eyelids, like thick syrup, dripped onto his cheeks, smothering into darkness…

Tick Tock…

LX flash of mother in picture frame.

ERNEST: Tick Tock…

LX flash of mother in picture frame.

ERNEST: Tick Tock…

LX flash of mother now standing behind ERNEST.

21. THOMAS' WAR MEMORY

'THOMAS' THEME' – *played on harmonica by THOMAS.*

CHORUS 2: Thomas had seen death before. Many times, it is the price of going to war.

CHORUS 1: But death is a strange creature, sometimes it will let you pass by freely and others it leaps upon your back, forcing you to carry it until you can walk no further before dragging you down into the mud with it.

Bullet hole lights in THOMAS' boxes come on. We hear loud SFX of gunfire made by CHORUS 1 and CHORUS 2.

THOMAS: He remembered shivering in the dark ruins of a derelict building as an enemy patrol searched for him and the remains of his unit.

He remembered the moon shining on the face of the young private whom they found in the room next to him.

The harsh sounds of the words they shouted at him…

CHORUS 1 shouting SFX.

THOMAS: Words he didn't recognise but the meaning of which he understood.

He remembered the faltering sound of the boy's voice as he begged for

CHORUS 2: Help! Mercy!

THOMAS: He remembered clutching his military issue
handgun, it feeling heavy and alien in his shaking hand.
He remembered trying to move, to stand, to act.
He remembered the moment it started to snow, a flicker of
beauty amidst the horror.
He felt the snowflakes falling upon his face.
He remembered the sound of a gunshot.
Then silence.

Lights change.

'ERNEST'S THEME' – *played slowly.*

22. ERNEST STARES AT THE PORTRAIT, THOMAS STARES AT ERNEST, MEMORIES OF MOTHER

SFX – Cello shriek.

CHORUS 4: With a jolt, Ernest sat bolt upright in his chair.
His heart crashing against his chest like a drowning man
hammering at the surface of a frozen lake.

ERNEST: His mother's face stared back at him from the wall.

CHORUS 2: Memories dug at Ernest's skull like a hatchet, guilt
and fear pierced his spine like poison-filled incisors. He
forced some air into his shallow lungs.

CHORUS 3: He couldn't raise his eyes to meet hers. Though he
could feel them upon him.

*We hear footsteps, from the back of the auditorium a hooded figure
starts descending towards ERNEST.*

CHORUS 2 AND 4: He saw the shine of her perfect patent
leather shoes, the familiar sight of the hem of her dress, her
stockings beneath.
Click… click… Click…
Heel on hard wood.
Click…click…

The footsteps continue as the figure gets closer to ERNEST.

CHORUS 3: Ernest tried to tear the unwanted thoughts from his head, pulling at them, one by one like strands of hair. But as he pulled they just got longer and longer.

CHORUS 2 AND 4: Click, click...

CHORUS 3: He closed his eyes and braced himself for an impact.

MOTHER: But it didn't come, the heels of her shoes clicked on the hard wood floor as she turned and walked away.

ALL CHORUS: Click click
Scratch scratch
Knock knock knock
Tick tock
Click click
Scratch scratch
Knock knock knock
Tick tock

CHORUS 3 pushes ERNEST out of his chair. CHORUS 2 stands behind portrait. Lights change.

23. BLOOD SPREAD

CHORUS 3: Ernest couldn't help but notice that over the past few days the pigment seemed to be draining from his apartment. The carpet, the wallpaper, had all slowly started losing their colour, and now they appeared white. Pure white, like virgin snow.

CHORUS 4: Even the portrait of his mother had started to change. Her face had become paler, as if a terrible fright had caused it to turn pure white and now you could barely make her out against the stark canvas.

ERNEST: He stared at the painting.

CHORUS 4: The eyes bore into him.

CHORUS 3: He couldn't be sure but it seemed to be moving, almost imperceptibly.

ERNEST: It seemed to breathe.

CHORUS 4: Ernest's heart faltered as he realised the face he was now staring at was not that of his mother, but of a young woman. A young woman with a shock of white hair.

The picture slowly starts to come to life.

CHORUS 3: The eyes of the poor white woman in the picture started to widen and her breath began to quicken, as she tried desperately to fill her lungs but could not.

The picture screams.

CHORUS 4: He ran to the wall, tearing down the painting. But as he did, he revealed the scarlet stain behind it.

As ERNEST tears down the picture it is replaced by a swirling blood spot which starts to grow in front of his eyes.

CHORUS: Scratch, scratch, scratch,

CHORUS 3: He watched as the mark bleed across his wall, spreading like a cancer.

CHORUS: Scratch, scratch, scratch,

ERNEST: Ernest closed his eyes

CHORUS 2: A shock of red on white.

ERNEST: Her face, her skin.

CHORUS: Scratch, scratch, scratch,

CHORUS 3: He felt the hot liquid under foot.

Red lights under floorboards on.

CHORUS: Scratch, scratch, scratch,

CHORUS 4: Red, blood, everywhere,

CHORUS: Scratch, scratch, scratch,

CHORUS 2: Consuming the walls and the ceiling and the floor, crawling up them like a swarm of fire-ants.

Red light fills the stage.

CHORUS 3: The whole room, the whole apartment, drowning in blood.

CHORUS: Scratch, scratch, scratch,

CHORUS 2: Scratches echoed through him from every wall of the house.

ERNEST: Where is she?

CHORUS 3: He raced to his kitchen, dragged open the drawer and pulled out the knife.

CHROUS 4: He heard her breath, felt it upon his face.

CHORUS: Scratch, scratch, scratch,

CHORUS 3: The hot-house flowers attacked his senses.

ERNEST: He couldn't breathe.

CHORUS 3: He rushed to the window and flung it open.

Sudden light change from red to white.

SFX of outside.

CHORUS 2: Ernest felt the icy breeze on his cheek and filled his lungs, gulping at the fresh night air, his shaking hands clutching the knife as the moon's rays shined down upon it.

Lights change.

'THOMAS' THEME'

24. THOMAS GOES TO ERNEST'S APARTMENT

'THOMAS' THEME'

THOMAS: Thomas Thistle was stirred from his uneasy slumber.

THOMAS: Something was waking him, calling to him.
Something, he felt it, a light shining upon his face –
A signal? A warning? A cry for help?
The light that he had seen before, the light…
…from the night that she died.
He looked up at the dark window of the dark building.
Thirteen up, seven across.
Something sparked inside his chest, a determination. He
dragged himself to his feet grabbing at the grabbing at the
handle of his gun, the gun that had never been fired.
He lurched out of his room and started limping across the
space between the two buildings, ignoring the shrieking
pain in his leg as metal chewed at the flesh and muscle.
He opened the doors and started climbing the stairs,
hammering his stick down hard upon each step.
One, two, three, four, five, six, seven, eight, nine,
ten, eleven, twelve,
thirteen floors up.
He counted the doors…one, two, three, four, five, six…
Six…six…six…

ERNEST: Ernest heard the footsteps; he clutched his knife
tightly in his palm. She is coming!

THOMAS: Thomas gripped the handle of his gun with a vicious
intent, as if trying to choke the life out of it,
Seven across, on the corner.
BANG BANG BANG!

ERNEST: She is here!

Lights change.

'BLOOD THEME' – *the structure is turned as ERNEST stands upon
it, ripping down the wallpaper and the planks to open the cavity.*

ERNEST: Ernest couldn't bear it any more.
In desperation he started clawing at the wall, scratching at

the paper with his fingernails, scraping at the wood, pulling out the nails, prising up the boards.

Trying to find her, to reveal her, to set her free!

THOMAS: **BANG BANG BANG!**

ERNEST: Ernest stared into the blackness.

THOMAS: **BANG BANG BANG!**

ERNEST: Ernest forgot to breathe...

THOMAS: **BANG BANG BANG!**

The noise builds to a climax before suddenly cutting out. LX flash on ERNEST – silent scream.

Lights change.

25. THOMAS ENTERS ERNEST'S APARTMENT

LX – torchlight only.

THOMAS: The scream that Thomas heard from behind the door would stay with him for the rest of his life. Even amidst the horror of war he had not heard such a sound emerge from another human being. It filled him with fear and horror and pity.

CHORUS 4: Unable to battle with his morbid curiosity, he slowly forced open the door and raised his gun. The first thing that hit Thomas was the smell.

CHORUS 2: Slowly the moon's rays seeped into the room and Thomas began to make out the shape of Ernest Hemel, lying motionless on the floor. Next to a large portrait of a pale lady.

THOMAS: Thomas saw a shock of white hair upon Ernest's head and an expression on his face that chilled him to the core.

CHORUS 4: Ernest's hand twitched involuntarily. Thomas saw the flash of the knife. He lowered his gun, it would remain unfired.

Lights change.

26. ASYLUM 4

'ASYLUM AMBIENCE'

NURSE: It's like he'd seen a ghost. Maybe he had.

EDGEFORD: …and what about the young girl? The one Thomas Thistle had thought he'd seen killed.

NURSE: The girl was fine, they found her in his mother's room. Tucked up in bed, sleeping. A single puncture wound, near her spine that had been dressed and treated, apart from that…

EDGEFORD: And his mother?

Lights change.

27. THOMAS SEES ERNEST'S MOTHER IN WALL

THOMAS: Thomas's eyes followed the shaft of moonlight as it crept up the wall, illuminating a spot where the wallpaper had been torn away and the planks of wood forced aside, to reveal a cavity.

ALL CHORUS: Tick tock tick tock tick…

CHORUS 4: Thomas forgot to breathe as through the darkness he saw the decaying body of Ernest's mother, her hands and face contorted into their final expressions of fear and desperation.

CHORUS 2: The moon's rays rested gently upon her face, at peace.

THOMAS: Thomas closed his eyes.

Lights change.

28. ASYLUM 5

'ASYLUM AMBIENCE'

NURSE: She'd been there for years, hidden in the walls. Stabbed her in the back. His own mother. They reckon she was still alive for days after he'd buried her. Neighbours reported scratching in the walls around the time that she died, but they just thought it was rats and then when it stopped a few days later they thought no more about it. Poor woman.

Lights change.

29. ERNEST IN ASYLUM CELL

'ASYLUM AMBIENCE'

ERNEST's face is lit only by the light from the small hatch of the Asylum door.

ERNEST: Tick tock tick tock tick tock...Ernest sat in his cell staring at the picture of his mother as the picture stared back. He tried to ignore the scarlet stain that glistened around the outside of her frame and the sound of scratches that echoed in his ears.
She belonged to him!

SFX of cell door hatch slamming shut. Blackout. Silence.

END.

Gwendoline Bertram's Lunar Incantations,
Will Teather, 2011, Acrylic on panel, 52 x 62cm

THE VAUDEVILLAINS

Pig design sketch, 'Golden Cleaver' – Sam Wyer

Foreword

Long-time Les Enfants Terribles collaborator and composer Tomas Gisby and I had been toying with the idea of writing a musical for a while. Through *The Terrible Infants* and increasingly in *Ernest and the Pale Moon*, our passion for live music in our work was growing and the scores were becoming more and more prominent.

Music can create a mood or a place so quickly, often more quickly than you can with words, which allows you to jump between locations and moods at speed. It can be, in effect, a guide which whisks your audience up and takes them along on their journey, telling them the moments they need to feel tense, happy or sad. This can be very appealing to a writer as it does half your job for you! In *The Vaudevillains* it allowed us the freedom to pack in quite a large number of different worlds and stories to its relatively brief running time.

Tom and I were immediately very attracted by the cabaret/ music hall conceit that forms the backbone of *The Vaudevillains*. We were keen to embrace this world but at the same time shoot it through with a strong narrative; therefore we needed a story which tied all our disparate acts together and so the murder -mystery seemed perfect: a framing device which allowed us to explore all the different backstories of the weird and wonderful acts at The Empire whilst still remaining pertinent to the central narrative. Creating these characters and working in this world was a real joy and did in many ways feel like the culmination of our work on previous productions. We viewed each song as a story. The thing that immediately struck me with putting words to music is that it allowed me to be a lot more direct, to cut straight to the meat as it were, which has quite a distilling effect in terms of the way you compose a story. Also, as someone fascinated by language, I enjoyed the exploration of how words behave differently when sung than when spoken – often landing our cast with near-impossible vocal tongue twisters to force their classically trained teeth around.

Published here is the libretto without the score, which is a bit like looking at a rainbow in black and white! However I do hope you can still get a sense of the anarchic fun of the piece and enjoy the stories within. I also hope that one day you will get to listen to Tomas's wonderful music too.

Oliver Lansley

Composer's Note

When Oliver and I created *The Vaudevillains* we wanted the subjects and themes to reach beyond its fictional home of The Empire music hall. During the show the setting quickly changes between the stage of The Empire and a variety of other intriguing locations, as the Acts' colourful backstories unfold.

Likewise, I wanted the music to have influences spanning further than the walls of Charlie's Club. Similar to the music that Neil Townsend and I composed for *The Terrible Infants*, the score draws on various genres, from jazz to classical, swapping styles to suit each of the tales of the Acts. Most importantly, I wanted to create some catchy melodies that an audience would find themselves humming as they left the theatre.

I hope you enjoy reading the libretto for *The Vaudevillains*, and I hope that one day you get to hear it sung too!

Tom Gisby

Co-Director's Note

It is very apt that these three shows have been published together in one volume. At first glance a Roald Dahl-esque family show, a Gothic noir ghost story and a Vaudeville musical might not seem that similar but these shows represented a time for the company where we were keen to explore a very wide variety of techniques; puppets, instruments, moving sets, live bands etc. The stories themselves play with structural narrative and as producers and creatives we wanted that to be reflected in how we brought them to life. As Co-director of *The Vaudevillains* and one of the key creatives of *The Terrible Infants*, I was always keen to try and tell the story in a simple but creative way – using puppets, bits of junk or whatever else was to hand. For *The Vaudevillains*, which was the company's first musical, I never saw it as a piece of musical theatre and was very keen to create a world that would work equally as well without song. It seemed a natural progression for the company to tackle a musical but the focus, as always, was the script and the story. For better or for worse, I had no preconceived ideas of how a musical should be presented; Oli's writing is pretty descriptive but at the same time allows for personal interpretations. The overriding aim I had with the show was to try and create a world of extremely varied, weird and wonderful characters that inhabit this strange club called The Empire. I kept thinking about the image of a group photo, posed outside The Empire club; Everyone looking equally bizarre yet bound together like a family. It was an exciting challenge to create that world, pull it all together and bring to life the fantastic music.

James Seager

Designing The Vaudevillains

Capturing the seedy spirit of music hall with a Les Enfants twist was both a challenge and a lot of fun! Our first incarnation of the show was required to work in a standard theatre environment and as a 'pop-up' piece for some more unusual venues (our fit up time at Latitude Festival 2010 was just 15 minutes!).

Despite this diversity of space we knew we still had to make 'The Empire' Music hall more than just a set but an extra character, and one worth killing for!

So we created a giant pop-up paper theatre, covered in strange macabre images and optical illusions. And inside that we built a large rotating box of tricks to be able to spontaneously change scenes without the bother of flying.

The box / cupboard / wardrobe / 'that bloody thing', as it was called on various occasions, came to life through the same economical use of space and material that made *The Terrible Infants* so slick and resourceful. However like *The Terrible Infants* and *Ernest and the Pale Moon*, these changeable sets only work due to the skilful and energetic performances put in by the cast who manipulate them.

Ten heavy-duty casters, a steel pivot, two concertina doors, two double doors, two secret doors, a rolling bill poster, a hidden rolling projection screen, pulley operated cinema drapes, and a shower curtain, all combined in various ways so that this 'box' was able to change from butchery competion to silent cinema to freezer to freakshow and more, in a matter of mere moments.

The costumes too had this multifunctional quality, telling the story through the layers they revealed. In the second incarnation of the show both the costume and set took on a more macabre twist, with the costume become bolder in colour and grotesquery, and the set moving more towards a callous woodcut in black, white and red, than the original more colourful 'toy theatre' style.

I could continue to tweak this show forever, and probably will, but there is one thing I feel I should point out to anyone who may wish to stage this production... Mr Punchy needs to be indestructable! Our Punchy was a repulsively reinvented 'Mr Parlanchin'; a popular, mass produced, ventriloquist's dummy from the late Seventies. We wouldn't change him for the world, but fake blood, sweat, and thirty-year-old plastic do not mix well when violently shaken numerous times... sometimes gaffa tape just isn't enough!

Thank you to my amazing team for all your hard work, Sadeysa GB, Bridget Mckee, Teya Lanzon, Josh Q, and my Brother Joe in his brilliant woodland workshop; you are all legends.

Sam Wyer

'Gaston' design concept – Sam Wyer

'The Cerberus Sisters' design concept – Sam Wyer

THE VAUDEVILLAINS
2010 – 2011

THE TIMES ★ ★ ★ ★ – CRITIC'S CHOICE

This is a perfect miniature musical...The show feels descended from the Sondheim of *Sweeney Todd*, its humour dark but invigorating; the violence is kept on a cheerful Hallowe'en-ish level and framed in affection for a time when music hall aimed to amuse working people at the end of a hard week...as twisted as barley-sugar...Undemanding   pleasure all the way... words fail me.

TIME OUT ★ ★ ★ ★ – CRITIC'S CHOICE

Its deliciously grisly sensibility is cohesively realised through inventive staging, beautiful costumes and design, lusty performances and rollicking music. They should make a killing.

THE TELEGRAPH – CRITIC'S CHOICE

The Vaudevillains is bursting with both atmosphere and talent... strikes me as a cult hit in the making.

THE GUARDIAN

Its clever twisted gothic style, all skulls beneath the flowers, has the makings of a little fringe cult... murderously good fun.

BRITISH THEATRE GUIDE ★ ★ ★ ★ ★

Less a performance and more an event to be remembered... From a jaunty opening number straight through to the explosive finale, every moment was filled with laughs, wit and charm... the production never ceased to amaze. From musical conjoined triplets to the schizoid ventriloquist and trembling knife-thrower, the heady mix of old-school japery and genuine fun being had was addictively overwhelming.

FEST ★ ★ ★ ★ ★

Les Enfants Terribles don't do things in half measures. With a single performance of *Vaudevillains* at this year's Fringe, there was but one chance to impress a highly expectant crowd as they took over the Pleasance Dome for the night. They did not fail to impress… truly exceptional. The dark comedy tone, superb alliterative narration from The Empire's master of ceremonies and an engaging storyline that combines elements of the macabre, humour, murder-mystery and a plethora of plot twists combine to create a production that is fitting for its grand stage.

BROADWAY BABY ★ ★ ★ ★ ★

Ladies and gentlemen, please put your hands together for Les Enfants Terribles's exquisite world-class exclusive vaudeville extravaganza… Beautifully paced, the murder mystery framework gives the usual vaudeville format a deeper sense of motion and allows the magic, miming and freak-showing that is par for the course in vaudeville to take on new significance… as inspiring as it is entertaining. Les Enfants are a force to be reckoned with.

HAIRLINE ★ ★ ★ ★ ★

The Vaudevillains is a superlative production from the best theatre group to ever grace the Edinburgh Fringe. Celebrating their tenth year, Les Enfants Terribles has surpassed its own excellent standards, making *The Vaudevillains* perfect in every possible way.

LONDON FESTIVAL FRINGE ★ ★ ★ ★

What is apparent throughout this all-singing, all-killing romp is the joy of the artistry behind it. The creators have fastidiously presented a beautiful and grotesque little music box for us… solidifies this company as one that is worthy of a watch indeed.

EDINBURGH SPOTLIGHT ★ ★ ★ ★

The atmosphere before *The Vaudevillains*, Les Enfants Terribles' one-off show at the Pleasance Dome, was more like being at a rock concert than a theatrical production. After presenting much-loved and critically-acclaimed shows such as *The Terrible Infants* and *Ernest and the Pale Moon* at previous Fringes, it is easy to understand the devotion from those who lap up their macabre and grotesque patchwork, sewn together with cleverly written and excellently played music... a marvel worthy of the Victorian music hall superlatives used by the piece's compere. As *The Vaudevillains* drew to a close and its mysteries revealed, we were present at the birth of another deliciously dark and twisted classic from Les Enfants, and one that is most definitely five-star material.

'Ray the Blade' design concept – Sam Wyer

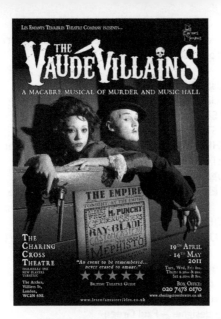

An early version of *The Vaudevillains* was performed by The Surrey Youth Theatre, directed by Angela Hardcastle, under the title *Charlie's Empire* at the Electric Theatre in Guildford in July 2010.

The Vaudevillains officially premiered at Latitude Festival in 2010 before a one-off performance which turned the entire Pleasance Dome into The Empire Nightclub for one night only on the 16th of August 2010 during the Edinburgh Fringe Festival.

> The Cast were:
> CHARLIE – Keith Hill
> COMPERE – Oliver Lansley
> MEPHISTO – Sue Appleby
> RAY THE BLADE – Marcus Ellard
> ALBERT FROG – Anthony Spargo
> MR PUNCHY – Himself
> THE CERBERUS SISTERS – Rachel Dawson, Jenny O'Neill, Catriona MacKenzie
> GASTON GASTEAU – Philip Oakland
> PAM CUSHION/NURSE WRETCHED – Charlie Mudie
> DR HANS FREAKIT – Tomas Gisby

The show was subsequently developed and performed at The Charing Cross Theatre, London in 2011.

The Cast were:
CHARLIE – Keith Hill
COMPERE – Oliver Lansley
MEPHISTO – Elizabeth Marsh
RAY THE BLADE/DR HANS FREAKIT – Trevor Jary
ALBERT FROG – Anthony Spargo
MR PUNCHY – Himself
THE CERBERUS SISTERS – Rachel Dawson, Alice Anthony,
Robine Landi
GASTON GASTEAU – Philip Oakland
PAM CUSHION/NURSE WRETCHED – Rebecca Bainbridge

Co-Directors – James Seager and Elgiva Field
Musical director – Candida Caldicott
Designer – Sam Wyer
Lighting designer – Paul Green

Note. For the original version of the show costumes were designed by Anna Bliss Scully, but for the transfer to The Charing Cross Theatre costumes were redesigned by Samuel Wyer with assistance from Sally Higginson

Vaudevillains proscenium arch design – Sam Wyer

Characters

CHARLIE

The Empire's owner

COMPERE

The Empire's compere

MEPHISTO

A Magician – Note. Mephisto is a woman
dressed as a man but this should not be obvious
to the audience

RAY THE BLADE

A knife thrower

ALBERT FROG

A Ventriloquist

MR PUNCHY

Albert's dummy

THE CERBERUS SISTERS, LA, DE and DA

burlesque Siamese triplets

GASTON GASTEAU

A mime. – Note. Gaston barely has any lines
throughout the show (as he is a mime), but it
is essential to always find ways of keeping him
involved and part of the action

Note. In each of the character's stories other characters appear. These can either be assigned to the actors playing the parts above or to members of the chorus/ensemble should you have one.

OTHER CHARACTERS

PAM CUSHION
Ray's assistant

DR HANS FREAKIT
A slightly crazy German Doctor, who appears in several of the character's stories

NURSE WRETCHED
A wicked Nurse who torments Albert

When ENSEMBLE is used the lines can be distributed to whoever you believe is best suited. ALL refers to the group singing as a whole.

Suitable lines in group songs may also be re-distributed to chorus/ensemble members to suit staging requirements.

'The Compere' – Josh Pharo

The Empire Music Hall.

Overture.

A spotlight appears on the empty stage, it searches around for a few moments, looking for something. Eventually it finds our COMPERE, somewhere in the auditorium. Throughout his speech he makes his way towards the stage.

COMPERE: Ladies, gentlemen, bachelors et bachelorettes,

Lovers, loners, husbands, wives,

mistresses, spouses, bits on the side,

old folk, cold folk, fat folk, thin folk,

broke folk, bloke folk, cannot take a joke folk,

folk who might have just awoke or the like the occasional smoke… folk,

those who wear a cloak folk or buy their clothes bespoke, folk.

folk who like a runny yolk or when they bathe they like to soak

folk recovering from a stroke or those whose favourite tree is… birch! Folk

To the middle-class 'Hello'

To the working-class 'A'wight'

From the looks of you we're not graced with the upper class tonight

To all the little children, Shouldn't you be in bed?

To all the old and ancients, Shouldn't you be dead?

To artists and accountants,

butchers, bakers and candlestick sellers

Cooks, crooks, dancers, docs

Ecologists, economists, farmers, gynaecologists

Historians and harpists

Ironmongers, judges, journalists

Karate instructors, labourers

Maids, magistrates and milliners

Nuns and nannies, novelists

Optometrists, oncologists

Pastors, painters, queens and quilters

Restauranteurs and retailers

Saxophonists and sailors

Tailors, tinkers

Undertakers,

Veterinarians and vegetarians

Weathermen, xylophonists, yodellers and... zoologists

Welcome... To The Empire!

There is a flourish and the lights explode on to the stage.

They hold their 'name boards' – after they are introduced they all ritualistically place their name boards in the Bill holder at the side of the stage to form The Empire's Bill.

ALL: Tonight at The Empire,

We'll excite at The Empire,

We'll burn bright and delight,

Tonight...

During this the COMPERE slowly stalks around the acts, building the anticipation.

COMPERE: Freaks, showmen, comely women

lend me your cheers and allow me to introduce tonight's bill!

As he speaks the acts all start to vocalise and encourage him, cheering, heckling, wolf-whistling, etc. This whole section should be rowdy, bawdy and interactive, a slight bear pit element, building anticipation and giving us a chance to 'meet' all of our characters. (Note. These need to feel very different to the later introductions.)

For RAY the cast perform their own drumroll by drumming their hands, on legs, set, each other, they make the requisite 'oohs' and 'aahhs' after each comment, etc.

He can split a nat's nut from fifty yards

He can cut through steel like he's cutting cards.

There's no target he can't hit,
he's almost sharper than my wit
In France they call him as *La Razor*,
In Germany, *Die Klinge*,
But here, we know him as Ray the Blade!!!

The rest of the cast cheer. The COMPERE moves on to the CERBERUS SISTERS. The cast wolf whistle and cheer.

Ladies lock up your fellas and throw away the key, for there is simply no escape from what you are about to see.
Not so much a feast of flesh as an all you can eat buffet.
Six eyes, three noses, half a dozen thighs and thirty toes, six peaks and twelve cheeks
They must be nature's finest freaks.
They say two heads are better than one, well a triple header's as good as they come.
These girls'll make it so hard…
…For you to forget them, you'll wish you never met them.
They're the world's only Siamese Striplets they are… The Cerberus Sisters!

The cast cheer enthusiastically. The COMPERE moves on to GASTON. The cast all 'shh' each other, miming their appreciation.

They say actions speak louder than words well his actions sing like birds.
His movements shall so engross,
You'll soon find Shakespeare quite verbose.
You'll think Tolstoy talks too much and Wordsworth is a little wordy.
He's sure to leave you as speechless as he is, he's the maestro of mime. Please make absolutely no noise whatsoever for the gestictacular Gaston Gasteau!

The cast cheer. The COMPERE moves on to MEPHISTO.

Some say that his parents were a wizard and a witch,
and they abandoned him as a baby in a basket in a ditch.

Others say he did a deal with some kind of devilish beast,

Or perhaps he was taught by a china-man whilst travelling the Far East.

There's just one thing we know is true

Whatever your conclusions,

Is that The great Mephisto shall astound you with his masterful illusions!

MEPHISTO does a brief but visually impressive trick and the rest of the cast cheer and coo accordingly. The COMPERE moves on to ALBERT.

Our final act is a ventriloquist…

Nothing rhymes with ventriloquist

Least but by no means last,

the final member of our cast

He can throw his voice

Like he's throwing a dart

He's the master of his art

he's sure to split your sides apart.

It's the deliciously demented duo

Albert Frog and Mr Punchy!!

The cast all start going crazy with excitement. The sound builds to a peak. The COMPERE has to do everything he can to quiet them down. Eventually he hushes them, the lights lower, very quietly we have…

The curtain's up, the stage is set,

Prepare for a night you'll never forget,

Our acts are primed and ready to go,

Without further ado let's get on with the show!

Suddenly the music kicks in, the lights come up and the opening number begins.

'TONIGHT AT THE EMPIRE'

ALL: Tonight at The Empire,

We'll excite at The Empire,

All your troubles will be out of sight,

Tonight at The Empire.
Stay all night at The Empire,
'Til first light at The Empire,
It's impossible to be uptight…
at The Empire.

ALBERT: There'll be gags to amuse,

MR PUNCHY: There'll be bucket-loads of booze,

COMPERE: There'll be songs and there'll be dance,

MEPHISTO: There'll be tales of wild romance.

RAY: There'll be talent to inspire,

CERBERUS SISTERS: There'll be beauties to admire,

COMPERE: Rush for a decent seat,
'Cos you're in for such a treat.

ALL: Come with us, come inside
Strap yourself in for the ride,

BOYS: You don't need to wear a suit,
We are a house of ill repute.

CERBERUS SISTERS: And us girls we are such cuties
Blessed with truly natural beauty.

COMPERE: Everything you see is real,
you don't believe me, have a feel!

ALL: Tonight at The Empire
We'll excite at The Empire
All your troubles will be out of sight
Tonight at The Empire.
See our bill at The Empire
We will thrill at The Empire
Show such skill, all your dreams we'll fulfil at The Empire.

MEPHISTO: I'll perform magic tricks without match,
and my world-famous bullet catch.

ALBERT: I'll tell jokes and try to be funny,
 Whilst not moving my mouth…

MR PUNCHY: …'oh shut up you dummy!'

RAY: I'll throw knives at my lovely assistant
 And hope my aim remains good and consistent.

CERBERUS SISTERS: We'll perform a sensational strip
 even though we're all joined at the hip…

All look at GASTON, but he just shrugs… 'I'm a mime'.

ALL: Tonight at The Empire
 We'll excite at The Empire
 All your troubles will be out of sight… at The Empire.

COMPERE: Got no cash, what the heck!
 We can always take a cheque
 You can stick it on your plastic as you trip the light
 fantastic.

ALL: Come and join us don't delay,
 be part of our little soiree,

MEPHISTO: we have the finest cabaret,

ALBERT: so many characters to play,

CERBERUS SISTERS: so many cans of cheap hairspray,

RAY: such a magnificent display,

COMPERE: Sometimes it gets a bit risqué, but that's ok, be led astray, we'll swing and sway, just come and play, yes every day, hey why not stay…

ALL: …we even do a matinee!
 Tonight at The Empire
 We'll excite at The Empire
 All your troubles will be out of sight…
 At The Emp…

Interruption, the band peters out…

CHARLIE: Stop, Stop!

> You won't get away with this!

> I'm gonna tell them all about what you did…

COMPERE: Ladies and gentlemen, the owner of The Empire…

> Charlie!!!

> You can see why they call him Champagne Charlie…

He makes drunken gesture.

Come on Charlie, let's get you off…

He nods and the music starts up.

ALL: Tonight at The Empire,

> We'll excite at The Empire,

> All your troubles will be out of sight,

> Tonight at The Empire.

> Stay all night at The Empire,

> 'Til first light at The Empire,

> It's impossible to be uptight…

> All your troubles will be out of sight,

> We'll burn bright and delight and take flight…

> …at The Empire.

Pyrotechnic bang for ending. Everyone is in position.

Suddenly there is a blackout – we hear a scream, followed by the sound of lots of commotion. Lots of screams, etc.

Suddenly the sound stops and the lights snap up quickly to reveal the dead body of CHARLIE, in the middle of the stage and all of the different acts standing over him, holding what is their potential weapon in a slightly threatening manner, e.g RAY/knife, MEPHISTO/ gun, etc.

The classic whodunnit image.

The cast then realise they are being watched, they all look up at the audience guiltily and smile awkwardly, standing up straight, trying to look innocent.

In the music a rhythmical pulse like a life support machine starts, the COMPERE moves to the front.

'Whodunnit' – Alex Stephens

COMPERE: Nobody panic, don't be alarmed.

MEPHISTO: Is he moving?

ALBERT: Is he breathing?

COMPERE: Let's not get manic, let's all stay calm.

CERBERUS SISTERS: Is he ok?

RAY: Is he bleeding?

COMPERE: Stay in your seats, do not dismay, I'm sure that
everything will be ok.

The pulse flatlines.

MEPHISTO: He's dead.

COMPERE: Ah…

COMPERE inspects CHARLIE's body.

Poor old Charlie, stabbed in the back in his own Empire…

'WHY CHARLIE WHY?'

*The cast all look at each other suspiciously. The following song is
performed with thoroughly over-the-top sincerity – each one trying
to outdo the other in grief to prove their innocence.*

MEPHISTO: Who'd want Charlie dead?

RAY: Everyone loved Charlie.

ALBERT: Who'd want Charlie dead?

CERBERUS SISTERS: Our dear old friend Charlie.

MEPHISTO: Who'd want Charlie dead?
    If you'd met him you'd agree
    Just to know him made me grateful
    It was clear for all to see… that…

CERBERUS SISTERS: Everyone loved Charlie,
    Everyone loved Charlie,
    If you'd have known him you would too.

RAY: His heart was made of gold.

ALBERT: And he was prized by all he knew.

ALL: Why Charlie why?
  Why Charlie Why?
  Charlie why?
  Why Charlie Why?

COMPERE: He's been shot.

MEPHISTO guiltily hides the gun behind her back.

MEPHISTO: He was such a classy fellow.

COMPERE: He's been stabbed.

RAY hides the knife he is holding behind his back.

RAY: He would always have a smile.

COMPERE: And strangled.

The CERBERUS SISTERS pull off their feather boas and hide them behind their backs.

CERBERUS SISTERS: He was always in a good mood.

COMPERE: And hit over the head with a blunt object.

ALBERT hides his dummy behind his back, GASTON holds an imaginary blunt instrument behind his back.

ALBERT: He could make your life worthwhile.

ALL: Who'd want Charlie dead?
  If you'd met him you'd agree.

MEPHISTO: He was so patient and so kind.

RAY: He meant the world to me.

ALL: Everyone loved Charlie,
  everyone loved Charlie,
  If you'd have known him you would too.

CERBERUS SISTERS: He made the world a better place.

ALBERT: He was a hero through and through.

ALL: Why Charlie why?
    Why Charlie Why?
    Charlie why?
    Why Charlie Why?
    Why Charlie Why?
    Why Charlie Why?
    Charlie why?
    Why Charlie Why?

COMPERE: Well that's a lovely sentiment…
    if only it were true.
    You all wanted Charlie dead, it could be any one of you.

General protestations over the top of each other, the COMPERE continues to sing.

    Charlie knew all of you,

MEPHISTO: That's crazy!

COMPERE: He knew you all so well,

RAY: I loved the man.

COMPERE: In fact, too well, perhaps you'd say.

ALBERT: He was like a father to me.

COMPERE: He knew things about you all,

CERBERUS SISTERS: Why would we want to kill him?

COMPERE: Things you'd not want to give away.

GASTON mimes 'I loved Charlie'.

    Everyone has secrets, secret's that they'd kill to protect
    And that makes every one of you a chief suspect…

They all look at each other guiltily.

This morning each of you received a note, a note that Charlie wrote.

The COMPERE reaches into his pocket and pulls out a letter, he looks at the others who, one by one, sheepishly pull their letters out.

RAY: Dear Ray…

MEPHISTO: Mephisto

GASTON: (*Silently.*) Gaston

ALBERT: Albert

CERBERUS SISTERS: Girls

ALL: Tonight will be your last night at The Empire.
After the show, pack up your things, get out and go,
and never come back to The Empire.
Otherwise I'll tell the world
About what you did…
Lots of love,
Charlie

After a moment, the entire cast all descend into shouting accusations at each other, protesting their own innocence. This leads into the cast collectively accusing each other, there's real venom in their words.

You wanted Charlie dead.

MEPHISTO: He was such a nasty fellow.

ALL: You wanted Charlie dead.

RAY: He was always so hostile.

ALL: You wanted Charlie dead.

CERBERUS SISTERS: He was always mean and rude.

ALL: You wanted Charlie dead.

MR PUNCHY: He could make your life so vile.

ALL: Everyone loathed Charlie,

everyone loathed Charlie.

If you'd have known him you would too.

CERBERUS SISTERS: His heart was icy cold.

MR PUNCHY: He was despised by all he knew.

ALL: Die Charlie die!
Die Charlie die!
Charlie die!
Die Charlie die!
Die Charlie die!
Die Charlie die!
Charlie die!
Die Charlie die!

Yes we would have done it, if we could have done it, but we didn't done it…

LA: So who did done it…

DE: did it…

DA: do it…?

MEPHISTO: Who killed Charlie?

Blackout.

COMPERE: Ladies and gentlemen, we have quite a show for you tonight, allow me to introduce… the suspects!

We introduce each act, a roving spotlight passes over them as they all hold up their name boards like prison number signs in police mug-shots.

As they leave they slot their name boards into the Bill holder on the side of the stage to form the Bill.

The Great Mephisto with his blinding bullet catch, has he conjured up a magical murder?
Or did the sexy Cerberus Sisters commit a thrilling killing?

Perhaps the glorious Gaston has perpetrated silent slaughter?

Or did the Amazing Albert Frog with his little friend Mr Punchy finally deliver that killer punch-line?

Spotlight on the COMPERE.

But first up we have a real treat,

With a death defying feat,

Though I suggest those of a nervous disposition leave your seat.

Prepare to be impressed, he's a cut above the rest

He's the man who was born with a knife in his hand

The best in the land, just be careful where you stand.

Be impressed, be amazed, be very very afraid

And welcome to the stage the remarkable RAY THE BLADE!

Before the song kicks in we have a musical flourish. RAY starts performing the little rituals at the start of his act, he gets out his knives, demonstrates how sharp they are, maybe does a little trick or two, scaring the audience with it (oohs and aaahs from the cast).

When he's ready he gestures for his target.

RAY's assistant PAM is revealed, tied to a big target.

Drum roll, RAY builds the tension (as if it's a real knife throwing act).

He prepares to throw the knife, one, two, thr… – suddenly we cut to black and focus the light on PAM on the target.

She starts to sing…

'RAY THE BLADE'

PAM: Once there was a boy,

    a little boy who used to play with knives.

    He'd give the kids at school the fright of their lives,

    while they used to play with sticks

    he was busy learning tricks of the trade

    (as he learnt to use his blades).

'Ray the Blade' – Alex Stephens

This young boy's name was Ray,
and although he came from very slender means
Butchery was in his genes
What you'd call the family trade.
For his father had also held the blade,
and his father's father too
was a butcher through and through.
You might say it was fate,
that Raymond would inherit such a trait.
On his quest to be the best he'd grow greater than all.
With a knife in his hand
he became the greatest butcher in the land.

RAY re-appears – though this is a younger, more dynamic RAY.

RAY: When I was a boy
these hands were my gift
so steady and strong
so subtle and swift.
As smooth as a dolphin's fin,
as light as an eagle's wing,
as sharp as a honey bee's sting.
Strong like a bear claw,
tight like a crab claw,
fast as a cheetah's tale.
My hands were my holy grail!
With these I'll achieve my greatest ambition
and triumph at the Golden Cleaver Butchery Competition!

Suddenly the scene is broken and the ensemble come on with a big sign reading 'GOLDEN CLEAVER BUTCHERY COMPETITION', they then act as the crowd and the competitors.

ENSEMBLE: Chop chop,
Roll up,
grab yourself a blade.
Chop chop,

sign up,
can you make the grade…
Fortunes will be made.

A FRENCH BUTCHER enters.

FRENCH BUTCHER: 'Allo! I am Pierre
a butcher extraordinaire,
from Montpelier.
The opposition had best beware
of my special meaty gallic flair!

(*Spoken.*) I come to claim the cleaver!

A SPANISH BUTCHER enters.

SPAINISH BUTCHER: They call me El Meatador,
I come from El Salvador,
Never have I been beat before.
My opponents don't know what's in store for them.
I plan to wipe the floor with them.

(*Spoken.*) I come to claim the cleaver!

A GERMAN BUTCHER enters.

GERMAN BUTCHER: Mein namen ist Kurt, the best butcher in
Frankfurt.
The competition is cursed, my routine is so well rehearsed.
I plan to come first, with my speciality bratwurst.

(*Spoken.*) I come to claim the cleaver!

JUDGE: Butchers!
Prepare yourselves!

RAY: With my sword by my side
and the world at my feet,
I can do anything
with these powers of cutting meat.

JUDGE: GO!

All the BUTCHERS face the back and butcher away as the excited crowd sing.

ALL: Chop chop chop! etc.

RAY: As smooth as a dolphin's fin,
  as light as an eagle's wing,
  As sharp as a honey bee's sting.
  Strong like a bear claw,
  tight like a crab claw,
  Fast as a cheetah's tale!

JUDGE: Stop chopping! Gentleman, show me your meat!

Each of the BUTCHERS turn around one by one, the SPANISH BUTCHER reveals a piece of Spanish-looking meat platter, FRENCH BUTCHER reveals a French-looking steak, the GERMAN BUTCHER reveals some German sausages, and finally RAY…

He turns to reveal a large cut of beef, carved into something incredibly intricate and grand (Michelangelo's 'David' or similar).

The crowd go crazy! A celebratory moment when RAY is on top of the world and everybody loves him – reprise of the overture that introduced him.

RAY is awarded with the 'Golden Cleaver' Trophy.

Everyone goes nuts, they celebrate and descend into a mad, debauched party.

RAY: We had the biggest knees up
  that the town had ever seen,
  and gorged on every cut of meat that you could ever dream.

ALL: Fillet, shoulder, sirlion, shank,
  belly, brisket, loin and flank,
  T-bones, trotters, ribs and chops,
  they cleaned out the whole butcher's shop!

COMPERE: But when Ray went to see what food

was left in his cold stores,
he was chilled right to the core
as he crossed the fridge's floor,
by the click of the very heavy, thick and largely
soundproof metal door...

*We see one of the BUTCHERS from earlier sneakily locking RAY in
the fridge.*

ENSEMBLE: It wasn't till the following day the town became aware
their celebrated champion, Ray,
was now no longer there.
They found him curled up in a ball, shivering with cold...

RAY: and clutched tightly in my blue fingers
I grasped a cleaver made of gold.

PAM is wheeled back on, still attached to her target.

PAM: Poor Ray. His hands, once so steady and so strong
shook and shivered all day long.
Took months for them to stop.
And still he found it difficult to chop.
The best butcher of them all could barely hold a knife at all.

RAY: My hands are so weak and
riddled with pain,
I fear that I may never
butcher again.
As weak as a mouse's squeak,
as blunt as a mallard's beak,
as heavy as a hippo's physique.
Sluggish as a seaslug,
bugs like a bed bug,
Rattly as rattlesnake,
cursed by this dam-ned shake!

COMPERE: (*Spoken.*) Now Ray was fine 99% of the time,
but when you're a butcher that 1% counts...

Rhythmic chopping section.

(*Spoken.*) Poor Ray had too many fingers in too many pies…

CERBERUS SISTERS: (*Sung.*) …literally!

ENSEMBLE: And once the council got wind of this unpleasant situation,
Such a blatant disregard for health and safety regulations,
They shut his shop down without a moment's hesitation.
Leaving poor Ray in a state of total desperation.

We see RAY hit rock bottom. He rather over-dramatically trashes anything on stage he can find and sinks to his knees.

RAY: Whhhyyyyyyyyyy!

PAM: Ray was on the streets,
he had no food, few fingers, and no trade.
He had nothing left except his trusty blades.
But though he couldn't keep them still,
his hands retained their special skill.

COMPERE: One day as Ray sat on the street just playing with his knife,
He was spotted by a man who would go on to change his life.
When Charlie saw Ray's fingers spin his blades round so swift
He knew that he was witnessing a very special gift.

CHARLIE: Hello sir.

COMPERE: Charlie chirped whilst stubbing out his cigarette.

CHARLIE: I wonder if you'd fancy partaking in a little bet?

COMPERE: He grinned at Ray and reached into the pocket of his coat.
Then with a flourish produced a crisp and fresh 50 pound note.
He strolled across the street and pinned the note upon a door,
Then he fixed Ray with a stare and said…

CHARLIE: If you can hit it, then it's yours.

ENSEMBLE: Ray looked at the man in disbelief, then stumbled to his feet.
And fixed his eyes upon the note that was pinned across the street.
He looked down at his quivering hand with fresh determination
and declared…

RAY: I will win this bet and with it find salvation.

PAM: So he clenched his teeth and let his butcher's knife fly…

Repeat the build-up we had when RAY performed his knife throw at the beginning of the act. He throws the knife.

Spot on knife as it pierces the note (Effect).

COMPERE: (*Spoken.*) …and the whole street watched in awe as it landed right between her majesty's eyes.

Music comes back in.

And so his path was made,
Ray the butcher became Ray the Blade
on his quest to be the best he'd grow greater than all
with a knife in his hand,
he became the best knife thrower in the land.

Lights up on how we started the song with RAY aiming at his assistant.

RAY: With my sword in my hand, and the world at my feet
My gift has returned and my life is complete.

We return to real time, PAM is back on the target, RAY is taking aim.

PAM: Once there was a man,
A gifted man who used to play with knives.
His hands were strong again and they shivered no more.
But though Ray felt he was fine,
in the back of his mind, he lived in fear,

one day the shakes would re-appear…

As at the beginning RAY aims the knife… One, two…

COMPERE: For even though he was fine 99% of the time,
when you're a knife thrower that 1% counts…

Three… Blackout. We hear PAM scream.

*Lights fade up on RAY with his head in his hands, the COMPERE
carries the body of PAM off of the target. CHARLIE stands behind RAY.*

CHARLIE: Don't you worry Ray, we'll find you a new assistant,
this'll be our little secret…

Lights fade down, spotlight fades up on the COMPERE.

COMPERE: Who'd want Charlie dead…?
Ray the Blade ladies and gentlemen!
If anybody's interested he needs a new assistant for his act?
If you're lucky you may even get to the end with
everything intact.
Sadly his condition's slightly worsening with his age.
But don't you worry as there's plenty more room left under
the stage.

Cymbal crash.

But that's our little secret…

He bangs the stage with his foot.

Next up on the bill,
They're here to thrill, they're dressed to kill,
for your entertainment pleasure,
they have talents beyond measure
so please put your hands together.
They're sexy, they're chic and they've got a rather nasty
streak…
The three, the only, the CERBERUS SISTERS!

166

Single spotlight on the three girls, singing angelically, we can't as yet see what they're wearing.

'OOPSY DAISY DADDY'

CERBERUS SISTERS: When mummy dear and daddy dearest tied that special knot,
they could never have anticipated getting what they got.
For when they hopped into their bed upon their wedding eve,
you simply would not believe
quite what they would conceive…

LA: (*Spoken.*) not one

DE: (*Spoken.*) not two,

DA: (*Spoken.*) but three,

LA: there was me

DE: and me

DA: and me

CERBERUS SISTERS: There was something a little different about these sweet young babes.
They say that some sisters are joined at the hip…

(*Spoken.*) well so are we…

LA: and at the stomach,

DE: and the ribcage,

DA: and the lungs…

Snare roll, they slowly reveal a little more flesh. Wolf Whistle. They raise their finger in protest, shake their heads and go back to being angelic.

CERBERUS SISTERS: But poor mummy dearest died,
As poor mummy dearest tried,
To push us three sweet babes between her sweet white thighs…

'He'd commited sordid acts with each of us behind our backs' – Alex Stephens

They start to click, we reveal their burlesque attire. Note. The CERBERUS SISTERS should be removing various items of clothing throughout the number as part of their 'act'.

We were left with dear old dad,

But dear old dad was such a cad.

He would call us freaks of nature.

He used to treat us real bad.

He would lock us in the cellar he would only feed us scraps,

just like poor old Cinderella, make us work till we collapsed.

(*Spoken.*) Cooking, cleaning, scrubbing floors, doing all the household chores,

Working till our hands were sore, and then he'd make us work some more…

But we always had each other,

we look after one another,

and we won't let any other

come between us…

LA: And then one day, poor old daddy passed away…

LA slowly takes off her feather boa and mimes strangling Daddy to the rhythm of the snare drum.

CERBERUS SISTERS: Oopsy daisy daddy,

daddy oopsy daisy,

You should take our advice.

Accidents can happen if you don't play nice.

Oopsy daisy daddy,

daddy oopsy daisy,

you best be warned.

Hell hath no fury like three women scorned.

So we joined Dicky's Circus,

where us three girls went to work as

Siamese sisters, circus freaks!
Daddy would have been so proud.
Good old Dicky took us in, and he managed all our affairs.
We became so fond of him, he was the answer to all our prayers.

(*Spoken.*) But tricky Dicky got too greedy, and the whole thing got too seedy

LA: Said he loved me,

DE: me,

DA: and me!

CERBERUS SISTERS: Affairs he managed with all three,
before we finally realised, old tricky Dicky's web of lies,
He'd committed sordid acts, with each of us behind our backs... literally.

But we always had each other,
we look after one another,
and we won't let any other
come between us...

DE: And then one day, poor old Dicky passed away...

DE slowly takes off her feather boa and mimes strangling Dicky to the rhythm of the snare drum.

CERBERUS SISTERS: Oopsy daisy Dicky,
Dicky oopsy daisy,
You should take our advice.
Accidents can happen if you don't play nice.
Oopsy daisy Dicky,
Dicky oopsy daisy,
you best be warned.
Hell hath no fury like three women scorned.

Then one day we met a surgeon,
who said he was on the verge of

a groundbreaking new technique,
A procedure that could split us apart.
But cutting edge surgery isn't cheap,
so earning lots of cash was essential.
That's when we met, good old Charlie,
and he finally saw our potential…

Blackout.

We hear CHARLIE introduce…

CHARLIE: Ladies and Gentlemen, Welcome to The Empire.
Tonight we introduce to you a very special new act.
You can only see them here folks,
The world's only Siamese Striplets
The Cerberus Sisters!

Fan/strip/burlesque dance routine.

We see money being thrown at them. Dollar bills rain down… Finally, when they have lots and lots of money, they get a volunteer up from the audience – it is the DOCTOR (would need to be dressed suitably to make this clear to the audience) – they hand him the cash.

He completes the final part of their striptease act by pulling out a large saw and using it to separate them. Should be playful and grotesque.

Blackout.

CERBERUS SISTERS: The procedure was a great success but Charlie, he was not impressed.

CHARLIE: 'What have you done!?'

CERBERUS SISTERS: rang in our ears,

CHARLIE: 'You've gone and ended your careers!
You were gifted with a fine physique that made you totally unique,
together you were truly blessed but now you're just like all the rest,
the same as all the girls I've hired,
so with regret, my loves, you're fired!'

CERBERUS SISTERS: *(Start v. slow, then accel.)*
We were all in total shock
and so we ran back to the Doc
'We've changed our minds!'
We cried in vain, you need to sew us up again.
He scoffed at us and shook his head.

DR: 'It can't be done!'

CERBERUS SISTERS: The Doctor said. 'We've nothing left, we got the sack.' We pleaded, 'Give our money back!'

DR: 'You should have thought of that before'

CERBERUS SISTERS: he growled at us and slammed the door.
But we always had each other,
we look after one another,
and we won't let any other
come between us…

DA: And then one day, poor old Doccy passed away… slowly and painfully.

DA slowly takes off her feather boa and mimes strangling the DOCTOR to the rhythm of the snare drum.

CERBERUS SISTERS: Oopsy daisy Doccy,
Doccy oopsy daisy,
You should take our advice.
Accidents can happen if you don't play nice.
Oopsy daisy Doccy,
Doccy oopsy daisy,
it's amazing what you can do
with a needle and thread and some super-strength glue.

They do a final reveal and we see that they are all attached once again, only this time it is very amateurishly done and quite grisly.

Blackout.

Spotlight on the COMPERE.

COMPERE: Ladies and gentlemen The Cerberus Sisters!

Once, twice, three times a lady, three times a charm,

Three times the men who sadly came to harm.

But we shouldn't make a fuss, we'll just keep it between us.

And now I think it's time,

To treat you to a bit of mime.

He really is sublime, in fact he's so good it's almost a crime.

He's the star of the show, please give a big Empire 'Hello!'

To the silent but deadly Mr GASTON GASTEAU!

Lights change.

We see old fashioned silent movie-style subtitles – they can either be projected or held up on boards.

The following sequence should feel like an old-school silent movie, complete with flickering light and stylised movement.

Note. Sentences in capital letters denote subtitles.

THE TALE OF GASTON GASTEAU

We see see various mimes in a line (like some sort of weird t'ai chi class) practicing their techniques, classic mime routines – walking the dog, opening a window, etc. A sign reads 'MIME SCHOOL – QUIET PLEASE'

PARIS, MANY YEARS AGO…

The teacher walks past, watching all the students, every now and then adjusting someone's technique, a mime on the end, ANTON is particularly good, the teacher praises him.

GASTON walks in wearing plain black clothes.

As he enters, the teacher puts up his hand to stop him. He then walks over, unlocks a mime door, opens it and nods at GASTON to come through it.

GASTON enters and speaks…

MY NAME IS GASTON – I WANT TO BECOME A MIME!

The teacher looks him up and down suspiciously, then gestures for him to show his skills.

GASTON mimes getting out a shotgun, loading it, aiming and firing, as he does we hear a loud squark and a dead bird drops from the ceiling. The mimes all look up at the bird, then at GASTON and burst into silent applause.

The mime teacher shakes GASTON's hands and welcomes him in.

GASTON TRAINED LONG AND HARD

We see all the mimes practicing as the teacher shouts out various mimes which they all do. ANTON and GASTON continue to look at each other, each trying to outdo the other.

WALK THE DOG!

TRAPPED IN A BOX!

PUTTING UP AN UMBRELLA...

They all mime putting up umbrellas

...IN STRONG WIND

The umbrella blows inside out.

BUT THERE WAS ANOTHER YOUNG MIME, ANTON, WHO WAS JEALOUS OF GASTON'S ABILITIES

The teacher calls ANTON to the head of the class and points at an empty space.

MOVE THIS BOX

ANTON moves to the imaginary box and struggles to try and lift it, but it's just too heavy, he gives up. The teacher points at GASTON, who comes over and after quite a struggle manages to lift the box into the air, he then proceeds to show off by spinning the box on his finger. The whole class applaud silently. ANTON fumes.

BUT WHEN THE DAY OF THE FINAL M.I.M.E.
EXAMS CAME...

SABOTAGE!

GASTON is putting on his gloves and warming up. ANTON appears, he looks at GASTON smiling, then goes to the imaginary door the teacher had set up, he waves at GASTON, then shuts the door, locks it and swallows the imaginary key. GASTON rushes to the door and tries to open it but he can't, he bangs on the door, ANTON laughs.

HA HA HA!

He exits, GASTON sinks to his knee, and shouts to the heavens.

NOOOOOOOOO

The board gets turned around.

OOOOOOOO!

FIFTEEN YEARS LATER

A worn looking GASTON takes off his beret, puts it down in front of him and performs a mime routine, a few people put in some money he smiles at them.

A man walks past holding a newspaper, the front page has a big picture of ANTON with the headline WORLD'S GREATEST MIME VISITS LONDON. The man drops the newspaper, it is ANTON standing with exactly the same look on his face as on the newspaper.

He puts a mime coin in GASTON's beret.

GASTON looks up and sees him, he points furiously...

YOU!

ANTON turns around and sees GASTON.

YOU RUINED MY LIFE! – I CHALLENGE YOU TO
A DUEL

He slaps him round the face with his white glove, then pulls out a mime sword.

The two men compete in a mime battle, starting with a sword fight, until it escalates into all kinds of mimed violence, (pulling guns, hand grenades, etc. out on each other. Note. This should be a well choreographed and comedic routine and the mimes must remain precise).

Finally GASTON defeats ANTON. ANTON falls to the ground and dies dramatically.

GASTON goes over and checks his pulse, ear to his chest, etc. He is dead. GASTON is suddenly wracked with guilt.

A crowd has gathered, CHARLIE walks through the crowd, starts speaking (out loud).

CHARLIE: Wow, you're the Great…

A subtitle appears.

WOW YOU'RE THE GREATEST MIME I'VE EVER SEEN!

CHARLIE looks up at it until it's stopped (or board holder walks off sheepishly), he then continues.

CHARLIE: You're the greatest mime I've ever seen.

But GASTON is wracked with guilt.

WHAT HAVE I DONE? I'M A MURDERER.

CHARLIE looks at the subtitle, then at ANTON.

CHARLIE: I think he'll probably be ok…

…A MURDERER!

CHARLIE looks to GASTON.

CHARLIE: I tell you what, you come and work for me, and we'll keep this as our little secret eh?

CHARLIE puts his arm around GASTON and leads him off. The crowd disperses leaving the body of ANTON alone on stage.

After a long beat ANTON sheepishly gets to his feet, brushes himself off, looks around and walks off.

Blackout.

Lights fade up on the COMPERE.

COMPERE: We're half way through our show tonight,
But there's still two acts to behold.
Two more talents to admire,
Two more secrets to be told.
We all have secrets, secrets that we'd kill to protect.
So allow me to introduce our next suspect…
Ladies and gentlemen, the magical, the mysterious, the Great Mephisto…

'SMOKE AND MIRRORS'

Spotlight appears on the MAGICIAN, looking down, but as his head is lifted we see it is a different person to who we've seen throughout the show.

He smiles and silently performs an illusion, making his beautiful assistant appear from his magic box.

When she appears we realise the assistant is who we thought was MEPHISTO all along.

Throughout the song we tell MEPHISTO's backstory, the whole thing has a slightly ghostly, occulty feel.

MEPHISTO: Remember you told me, one day we'd be famous,
the greatest magicians of all.
We'd be top of the bill, everyone would proclaim us
the best that the world ever saw.

Through the smoke and the mirrors we were having such fun,
but it's never the same when you know how it's done.

I laughed when you told me that we could be great,
we were just children with conjuring dreams.
I didn't believe that it could be our fate,

we practised all day, we made such a team.
Through the smoke and the mirrors we were having such fun,
but it's never the same when you know how it's done.
I watched as we grew and we polished our tricks,
and the audience grew too and became more transfixed.
I blushed when you said that you thought I was pretty,
and I held your hand tightly when we went to the city.
The bright lights, they made my eyes sting,
but with your arm around me I could do anything.
You made me feel strong, brought me out of my shell,
and before too long I was under your spell.

At this point our MAGICIAN re-appears in a cloak. He holds a mask as if for a masked ball. They embrace passionately. He puts a delicate eye mask on her, then puts on his own slightly more scary Venetian-style mask. They start to dance. As they dance she sings…

I sparkled with sequins as you sawed me in half.
My smile never faltered when I disappeared.
Each time I picked your card you could still make me laugh,
and when I levitated how all the crowd cheered…

The stage starts to fill with others in cloaks and masks. They all begin to waltz as if at a big masked ball.

Suddenly someone cuts in and MEPHISTO and the MAGICIAN become separated. The dance continues with MEPHISTO struggling to keep track of who the MAGICIAN is and getting more frustrated.

Eventually she is left alone on stage dancing with a cloaked figure. She removes their mask and the cloak disappears – revealing that there is no one inside.

Everything else cuts out and we hear a single woman's laugh.

A spotlight comes up on MAGICIAN canoodling with another woman.

MEPHISTO's heart sinks, she drops the mask. She is left alone on stage.

CHARLIE: And now, The Great Mephisto will perform his world famous, death-defying bullet catch!

The lights fade up. In silence we see the MAGICIAN preparing for the trick, putting on his blindfold, rolling up his sleeves. MEPHISTO just stands there holding the gun.

We see from her face she is holding back tears, her hand is almost shaking.

MEPHISTO: Remember you told me, one day we'd be famous,
the greatest magicians of all.
We'd be top of the bill, everyone would proclaim us
the best that the world ever saw.

Through the smoke and the mirrors we were having such fun,
but it's never the same when you know how it's done.

She fires the gun with a deafening bang.

Blackout.

Slowly the lights fade up and she is sitting at the front of the stage, mascara all down her face having cried her eyes out.

We watch her complete the transformation from assistant to MEPHISTO. Clothes, make-up, etc..

Slowly CHARLIE appears from the side of the stage, he is holding MEPHISTO's top hat, he walks over to her and silently hands her the hat.

MEPHISTO: (*Almost spoken.*) Through the smoke and the mirrors we were having such fun,
but it's never the same when you know how it's done.

She puts on the hat, until she is in exactly the same position the MAGICIAN was when we first revealed him. Blackout.

Spotlight up on the COMPERE.

COMPERE: And so we are nearing the end of the show,
with just one more act to go.
One more act upon the bill,
One more suspect left to grill,
One more secret left to spill,

One more reason left to kill.

Now I think it's fair to say that our next act's screw's a little loose.

He's some sandwiches short of a picnic, he's been drinking crazy juice.

He'll deliver killer lines, and hilarious quips and all the while without moving his lips.

He's really rather funny, but just don't call him a dummy, cos he might just boil your bunny.

Ladies and gentleman, he will amuse and entertain though he's clinically insane – it's dazzling and deranged Albert Frog and his little friend Mr Punchy…

Lights come up on ALBERT with his Dummy.

'BEFORE I MET YOU'

ALBERT: Before I met you I was always alone,
    had nobody with whom I could play.

MR PUNCHY: Before I met you I was left on my own,
    I never had nothing to say.

ALBERT: Before I met you…

MR PUNCHY: I was hollow inside.

ALBERT: Before I met you I was in lots of trouble,
    my life was hitting the rocks.

MR PUNCHY: Before I met you I was bent over double, and
    then you opened my box.

ALBERT: We do everything together,

MR PUNCHY: We're so synchronised.

ALBERT: The only thing we can't do is…

MR PUNCHY: …harmonise.

ALBERT: Before I met you…

MR PUNCHY: I was hollow inside.

ALBERT: But I wasn't always so content,
my earliest of years were spent
in a rather nasty place.
For a case of what they called

MR PUNCHY: 'schizophrenia'

ALBERT: and also a teeny weeny
amount of psychopathic rage.
Which I'd always kept at bay
until one fateful day,
when a bully at my school
who liked to make a fool
of me
made just one small joke too many…

(*Spoken.*) …but I don't remember anything after that… I guess
I just… snapped.

Suddenly the scene changes to reveal a mental asylum.

Before I met you I was in an asylum they were ready to
throw away the key.

MR PUNCHY: Before I met you, you were crazy and violent
but then you found solace in me.

ALBERT: Before I met you…

MR PUNCHY: I was hollow inside.

ALBERT: Before I met you, I was starved of affection, my life
was so full of complaints.

MR PUNCHY: Before I met you, you'd already been sectioned,
you had to be kept in restraints.

ALBERT is restrained on a gurney – 'Silence of the Lambs'-esque.

ALBERT: You gave me a reason, you gave me a choice.

MR PUNCHY: You gave me a hand you gave me a voice.

'Albert Frog' – Josh Pharo

ALBERT: Before I met you…

MR PUNCHY: I was hollow inside.

The DOCTOR appears.

DR: There was a pioneering Doctor,
who was convinced he could be fixed.
He tried all sorts of therapies,
All sorts of weird techniques and tricks…

We see a short montage of all the different types of therapy the DOCTOR suggests (the same DOCTOR that separated the triplets).

The DOCTOR stands there with a clipboard whilst the CERBERUS SISTERS, dressed as nurses, try various things and the DOCTOR shakes his head.

The NURSES…

Electrocute him.

DR: Nein.

Blow a foghorn in his ear.

DR: Nein.

Snap a sinister looking rubber glove on to their hand.

DR: Nein!
The Dr finally settled on 'Ventro Therapy'…

The NURSES hand him a dummy.

DR: 'Albert this is Mr Punchy'

ALBERT grins.

DR: – a groundbreaking new technique which involves
assigning the subject's multiple personalities
to a physical form, in this case a dummy.

MR PUNCHY: Hey watch who you're calling a Dummy!

The NURSES applaud the success and release ALBERT from his restraints.

DR: The progress was swift and the treatment went well.
But one day the Dr had to bid him farewell.

The DOCTOR leaves and is replaced by NURSE WRETCHED.

NURSE: …He was replaced by a terrifying nurse,
who thought the Doctor's new techniques were just
'perverse' and would only make him worse…

ALBERT: But when the nurse tried to take Mr Punchy away.
We decided to break out, to escape and run away.

*A short keystone cops-esque chase sequence, where CHARLIE ends up
hiding ALBERT from the NURSE.*

CHARLIE: Ladies and Gentlemen, Welcome to The Empire.
Tonight we introduce to you a very special new act.
This is his first ever time on stage so please give him a big
warm Empire welcome
Albert Frog and his little friend Mr Punchy!

ALBERT: Before I met you I was locked in my room and
nobody would be my friend.

MR PUNCHY: Before I met you I was locked in my box but it
turned out alright in the end…

*ALBERT and MR PUNCHY perform a short tap-dance routine,
taking it in turns to dance to the music.*

COMPERE: (*Spoken.*) But by some stroke of vicious, almost
inconceivable coincidence,
One day the terrifying Nurse turned up in The Empire's
audience…

NURSE: (*Spoken.*) 'This man's a raving loony, a danger to
society. Young man you are not well,

(*Sung.*) I insist, you come with me…'

The NURSE stands on the stage and orders him to follow her.

COMPERE: Albert felt a funny feeling that he couldn't quite ignore.

A sense of something snapping that he'd felt just once before.

But after that his memory failed and everything went black, As Mr Punchy shook his head...

MR PUNCHY: (*Spoken.*) I'm never going back!

ALBERT and MR PUNCHY start squaring up to the NURSE.

NURSE: What are you doing? Why is he looking me like that, stop, stop right there, Albert? ALBERT! Help, help! Somebody!

He chases the NURSE off stage, we hear the sound effects of her murder, limbs, heads, etc. appearing round the curtain as she tries to escape and keeps getting dragged back in. It should be very amusing and can be very over-the-top and escalate, with all sorts of bizarre sounds and objects popping round the edge of the curtain. An excessive amount of fake blood is recommended.

After the chaos dies down, ALBERT and MR PUNCHY return, MR PUNCHY should be covered in fake blood, silly and gory, not realistic.

ALBERT: Since I met you, my life has been great, I love being with you every day.

MR PUNCHY: Since I met you, you've really started to grate, I'm sick of you telling me what to say.

ALBERT: Since I met you my life couldn't have been asburder.

MR PUNCHY: And now I'm accessory to an awful murder.

ALBERT: Since I met you...

MR PUNCHY: it's been a hell of a ride.

ALBERT: Since I met you there's a smile on my face, I hope that we're always together.

MR PUNCHY: Since I met you I haven't had my own space now I'm reaching the end of my tether.

ALBERT: We'll always be together whatever comes to pass.

MR PUNCHY: I wish you would take your damn hand out my…

ALBERT: …Assssk anyone, before I met you, I was hollow inside.

MR PUNCHY: and since I met you,

ALBERT: it's been a hell of a ride!

Blackout.

A roving spotlight passes over the stage as we return to the moment before the back-stories began.

COMPERE: And now, please welcome the star of our show.
He's the man who we're all here for,
He's the last but not the least, it's just a shame that he's deceased.
He's The Empire's proud owner. It's… CHARLIE!

Finally the light settles on CHARLIE who lies dead on the floor.

The lights slowly fade up to the opening scene with everyone crowded around CHARLIE's body.

'WHY CHARLIE WHY – REPRISE'

ALL: Who'd want Charlie dead?

MEPHISTO: You must believe I didn't do it.

ALL: Who'd want Charlie dead?

RAY: I promise you it wasn't me.

ALL: Who'd want Charlie dead?

CERBERUS SISTERS: We are innocent you know it.

ALL: Who'd want Charlie dead?

ALBERT: I swear that I am not guilty

ALL: Everyone loathed Charlie

Everyone loathed Charlie

If you'd have known him you would too.

But I did not kill him.

Therefore it must be…

one of you!

Why Raymond why?

RAY: It was not me.

ALL: Why sisters why?

CERBERUS SISTERS: And not us three.

ALL: Why Albert why?

ALBERT: How dare you!

ALL: Mephisto why?

MEPHISTO: I'm not guilty.

ALL: Why Gaston why? Gaston Why?

GASTON protests his innocence. They start again.

Why (*Each say a different name.*) why?

Why (*Each say a different name.*) why?

Why (*Each say a different name.*) why?

(*Each say a different name.*) why?

Why Charlie why?

GASTON tries to get everyone's attention but they are all ignoring him, getting carried away with their song and their arguments and accusations. Eventually he grabs the gun which is in MEPHISTO's hand and fires it into the air, MEPHISTO looks at him.

MEPHISTO: I think he's trying to tell us something.

GASTON now acts out an elaborate series of charades to try and communicate with the group…

5 words, 1st word – 'HIT'

He acts out punching. They make several wrong guesses.

ENSEMBLE: …Punch? Smack? etc.

Before getting it.

HIT!

The game continues…

2nd word – 2 syllables, 1st syllable – 'WARS'

He acts out fighting and warplanes, tanks, etc.

They make several wrong guesses, all shouting different things over the top of one another, before they guess.

ENSEMBLE: Planes? Guns? etc. WARS!

2nd syllable – 'ANT'

He pretends to be an ant.

They continue to guess all shouting over the top of each other with different guesses.

ENSEMBLE: Alien? small? Tiny alien? etc. ANT!

3rd word – 2 syllables, 1st syllable – 'A'

He makes the shape of an A, they get it.

2nd syllable – KNEE

He points to his knee.

ENSEMBLE: Leg?…KNEE!

They try and guess…

ENSEMBLE: HIT WARS ANT KNEE…

They continue puzzled.

4th word – 'COUGH'

He mimes coughing.

ENSEMBLE: Singing? Sneeze? Lollipop?…COUGH!

5th word – 'BUS'

He tries to mime driving a bus.

ENSEMBLE: Driving? Car? Big car? Van? BUS!

They try and guess again.

ALL: HIT… WAS… ANT… KNEE… COUGH… BUS
HIT… WARS… ANTKNEE… COUGHBUS
IT…WAS…ANTKNEE…COUGHBUS.

ALBERT: IT WAS ANTHONY COUGHBUS!!!

Everyone gasps.

CERBERUS SISTERS: …Who's Anthony Coughbus?

GASTON can't take this any more, he breaks and shouts in a thick French accent.

GASTON: COME ON! WHAT IS WRONG WITH YOU
PEOPLE! LISTEN TO ME!!
IT… WAS…N'T… A…NY… OF… US… IT WASN'T
ANY OF US!
DO I HAVE TO SPELL IT OUT!?

They all look at him a little taken aback.

ALBERT: (*Aside.*) You know I had no idea he was French.

MEPHISTO: How do you know?

GASTON: Because, at the time of the murder we were all
together… onstage… doing the opening number!

They look at each other confused, he looks at the band and nods, they start up playing TONIGHT AT THE EMPIRE. They re-perform a section of the opening number, acting out their dance moves but instead of singing the lyrics they sing…

GASTON: So I was here.

ALBERT: You were where?

MEPHISTO: I was somewhere over there

RAY: I was here…

CERBERUS SISTERS: …and we were near

GASTON: Now it's all becoming clear.

ALL: Then we did the kicky thing, we waved our hands and did a spin.
Step-ball-changed into a line and danced this bit in double time.
Singing all in harmony, building to the finale…
and so we have the final clue, if we're all here then that leaves…

They hit their final pose. We hear the gunshot/pyrotechnic/drum hit moment when CHARLIE was killed. They open to reveal the COMPERE, standing there, holding his letter.

ALL: You…?

GASTON grabs letter and starts with 'sounds like', but MEPHISTO snatches it from him. They all read over each other's shoulder, as they did with the first letter.

MEPHISTO: This is the last will and testament
of Charles T Dreybourne Proud owner of The Empire.

ALL: Dear friends, I have something to tell you… I'm dying.
Sorry for how I've treated you all at The Empire…
I know that I, have been a bit… of a shit.
I hope one day you'll forgive me.
In my death I leave my Empire
to all the acts on the bill.

MEPHISTO: May it live on forever.

ALL: Lots of love,
     Charlie

*They all stare at the COMPERE. Suddenly the spotlight hits him,
he is introduced…*

CHARLIE: Ladies and Gentlemen, topping our bill for this
     evening,
     He's a liar and a cheat and a master of deceit
     I give you… your compere!

'BETRAYAL'

During the song the ENSEMBLE act out the story.

COMPERE: Many years ago, two men opened a club
     a club that would flourish and grow to be grand.
     They named it The Empire.
     It was the greatest in the land.

     The men were best of friends,
     until one of those friends
     betrayed the other, running off with his wife,
     crushing his world
     and ruining his life.

     But one thing that remained,
     in all of this despair,
     a bastard child, left from the affair
     A child, left in a broken man's care…

     That broken man's name was Charlie,
     and the bastard child was me… Betrayed.

     Charlie treated me,
     as if I was his own
     He brought me up like his own son,
     taught me everything
     about how the club was run.

191

Charlie needed me
To keep this place alive.
He put me to work from a very young age
made me help run the business
and put me on stage.

He told me every single secret belonging to each of you...

ALL: Betrayed...

COMPERE: And he promised me that one day his Empire
would be mine...
Betrayed.
Betrayal is the blade of the knife in your back
It's the whispered lie,
it's the heart that's black.
The kiss of a friend, as they watch you fall.
Betrayal is the most unkindest cut of all.

ALL: Betrayal.

COMPERE: But as the years went by,
As he looked into my eyes,
In those eyes he could see the eyes of my mother
But in my face he saw the face of her lover.

His bitterness took hold.
The drinking took its toll.
His heart became cold and twisted and black.
When The Empire needed him, Charlie turned his back.

The Empire would have crumbled...
If it wasn't for me...
Betrayed.

ALL: Betrayal is the blade of the knife in your back
It's the whispered lie,
it's the heart that's black.
The kiss of a friend, as they watch you fall.
Betrayal is the most unkindest cut of all.

COMPERE: Finally the Devil caught up with his man and
Charlie was sentenced to death.

The years of abuse had broken him down
he didn't have very long left.

The Dr gave Charlie just weeks left to live,
And Charlie came to me with letters to give.

But when I read what was inside I felt like such a fool
As my hard-earned inheritance was to be shared with you
all...

ALL: Betrayed.

Betrayal is the blade of the knife in your back
It's the whispered lie,
it's the heart that's black.
The kiss of a friend, as they watch you fall.
It's the most unkindest cut of all.

COMPERE: Betrayed. Betrayal.

Betrayed. Betrayal.

ALL: Betrayal is the blade of the knife in your back
It's the whispered lie,
it's the heart that's black.
The kiss of a friend, as they watch you fall.
Betrayal is the most unkindest cut of all.

COMPERE: But then I realised
as I read Charlie's will.
If I switched the letters
and told you to go,
The club could still be mine...
I'd be the only act left on the bill!

Betrayed. Betrayal.
Betrayed. Betrayal
Betrayed. Betrayal.
Betrayed. Betrayal

ALL: Betrayal is the blade of the knife in your back

it's the whispered lie,

it's the heart that's black.

The kiss of a friend, as they watch you fall.

It's the most unkindest cut of all.

Betrayal is the blade of the knife in your back

it's the whispered lie,

it's the heart that's black.

The kiss of a friend, as they watch you fall.

Betrayal is the most unkindest cut of all.

ALL: But Charlie found out during tonight's show…

The cast have all got themselves into their 'TONIGHT AT THE EMPIRE' positions. Suddenly the lighting changes and the song kicks in.

'TONIGHT AT THE EMPIRE REPRISE – MURDER AT THE EMPIRE'

Tonight at The Empire,

We'll excite at The Empire.

All your troubles will be out of sight

At The Emp…

Interruption, the band peters out…

CHARLIE: Stop, Stop!

You won't get away with this!

I'm gonna tell them all about what you did…

COMPERE: Ladies and gentlemen, the owner of The Empire… Charlie!!!

You can see why they call him Champagne Charlie…

He makes drunken gesture.

Come on Charlie, let's get you off…

He nods and the music starts up.

Suggestion: The cast all turn around to face the back as COMPERE leads CHARLIE off to give the impression we are now backstage. The rest of the cast continue with 'Tonight at The Empire' and the dance routine but facing the back of the stage. They sing very quietly. It is also much slower and clipped as if the whole thing is in slow motion.

ALL: Tonight at the Empire,

COMPERE: Why Charlie, Why?

CHARLIE: (*Spoken.*) I know what you did.

ALL: We'll excite at The Empire,

COMPERE: Why Charlie, Why?

CHARLIE: (*Spoken.*) I found the letters!

ALL: All your troubles will be out of sight,
　　　Tonight at The Empire.

COMPERE: Why Charlie, Why?

CHARLIE: (*Spoken.*) You'll never get away with this!

COMPERE hits CHARLIE with his cane.

ALL: Stay all night at The Empire,

COMPERE: Betrayed!

CHARLIE: After the show…

ALL: Till first light at The Empire,

COMPERE: Betrayed!

CHARLIE: …Get out and go.

ALL: It's impossible to be uptight…

CHARLIE: Otherwise I'll tell the world about what you did!

ALL: All your troubles will be out of sight.

COMPERE: Die, Charlie, die!

'Gaston Gasteau' – Josh Pharo

In desperation the COMPERE starts to strangle CHARLIE.

ALL: We'll burn bright and delight and take flight…

COMPERE: Die, Charlie, die!

COMPERE grabs RAY's knife and stabs him.

ALL: Tonight at The Empire.

CHARLIE: (*Spoken.*) You'll never work in this town again

The COMPERE grabs MEPHISTO's gun and shoots him.

Pyrotechnic bang for ending (covers gunshot). As this happens the chorus line breaks to reveal the dead body of CHARLIE in the centre of the stage.

CHARLIE falls to the ground into the position where his dead body has been throughout the show. The ensemble slowly crowd around him once more and look up at the COMPERE.

COMPERE: Ok, you got me, I killed Charlie.
You better call the boys in blue…

GASTON starts dialing a mime phone.

…And when they get here we can tell them all the things that you did too…

GASTON stops and puts down the phone angrily.

**'WHY CHARLIE WHY REPRISE
– YOU WANTED CHARLIE DEAD'**

COMPERE: You wanted Charlie dead.

MEPHISTO: You tried taking away our Empire.

COMPERE: You wanted Charlie dead.

RAY: It was your doing all along.

COMPERE: You wanted Charlie dead.

CERBERUS SISTERS: You're a villain and a liar.

COMPERE: You wanted Charlie dead.

ALBERT: What you did to us was wrong.

COMPERE: You wanted Charlie dead
 I'm sure you would agree.
 He was a pain in your behinds,
 He made your lives a misery.
 Everyone loathed Charlie, everyone loathed Charlie.
 And you all know you loathed him too.
 He was an absolute disgrace, he was villain through and
 through.

The Company turn on the COMPERE.

ALL: Tonight will be your last night at The Empire
 After the show, pack up your things,
 get out and go, and never come back to The Empire.
 Otherwise we'll tell the world
 About what you did…

COMPERE: Well that's a lovely sentiment,
 But I'm afraid I shall decline.
 As long as my name's on that bill
 The Empire's partly mine.

He gestures to The Empire Bill Poster.

(*Spoken.*) And I'm not going anywhere…
The show must go on!

*The other acts all stare at him, they close in on him, he looks
nervous.*

Blackout.

Spotlight up on MEPHISTO.

'TONIGHT AT THE EMPIRE – REPRISE'

We effectively start the show again.

MEPHISTO: The curtain's up, the stage is set,
Prepare for a night you'll never forget,
Our acts are primed and ready to go,
Without further ado let's get on with the show…

ALL: Tonight at The Empire,
We'll excite at The Empire,
All your troubles will be out of sight,
Tonight at The Empire,
See our bill at The Empire,
Dreams fulfilled at The Empire.
Show such skill, we will thrill,
watch us kill…

MEPHISTO: …ladies and gentlemen, welcome to The Empire.
I am the great Mephisto and tonight for the final ever time
I shall perform for you my world famous, death defying,
bullet catch!
And to assist me, please welcome my beautiful assistant!

*The COMPERE is wheeled on, tied to the target and gagged, he looks
panicked. MEPHISTO cocks her gun.*

ALL: Tonight at The Empire,
We'll excite at The Empire,
We'll burn bright and delight,
Tonight…

The COMPERE's eyes widen. Drum roll builds. Gunshot.

*The COMPERE's head flies back. After a few moments he slowly looks
up, before producing a bullet between his teeth and spitting it out.*

Blackout.

Band come in with reprise of 'TONIGHT AT THE EMPIRE'.